The Locality Commissioning Handbook

from vision to reality

Edited by

MICHAEL DIXON

TOPSY MURRAY

and

DAVID JENNER

Forewords by

SANDY MACARA

Chairman, British Medical Association

and

ANDREW WILLIS

Chairman, National Association of Commissioning GPs

RADCLIFFE MEDICAL PRESS

Radcliffe Medical Press Ltd
18 Marcham Road, Abingdon, Oxon OX14 1AA, UK

British Library Cataloguing in Publication Data

A catalogue record for this book is available from the British Library.

ISBN 1 85775 272 4

Library of Congress Cataloging-in-Publication Data is available.

Typeset by Advance Typesetting Ltd, Oxfordshire
Printed and bound by Biddles Ltd, Guildford and King's Lynn

Contents

Foreword

Someone has said that the darkest hour comes just before dawn. Scientifically this must surely be nonsense, but psychologically it has appeal, and it may serve as a metaphor for the National Health Service as it approaches its 50th birthday. The Thatcherite revolution represented by the 'reforms' and the imposition of the new GP contract in 1990/91 will provide a rich lode to be mined by future historians. I would hazard a prediction that they will view the last few years as just one stage – an aberrant yet formative one – in the evolution of the best health care system in the world.

Consider the outcome of the philosophy and strategy of an 'internal market' in the NHS, with its intended winners and losers. Doomed to failure in functional terms, it is now experiencing the inevitable obsequies. Equally, however, experience has shown the advantages in enhanced accountability and efficiency of the *structural* concept of a division of responsibility between those who assess the need and allocate resources accordingly and those who provide the care, whether in hospital or in the community. But these converse responsibilities need not constitute a 'split', nor need they be driven primarily by financial criteria as in the 'purchaser/provider' model. Indeed, the futility and fatuity of the divisive approach of the internal market have evoked the reaction of a return to the concept of a strategy for health and health care in defined populations. But it has to be a scientific strategy involving everyone concerned and through which resources can be allocated on the basis of properly assessed need on the one hand and effective care of high quality on the other. A new balance has to be struck between co-operation in deciding and agreeing how best to use the available resources, and competition for quality in the delivery of care.

The recognition of the need for this new strategy to be 'primary care-led' presents general practitioners with a golden opportunity to move on from sterile argument about fundholding to applying the lessons learned from it to devising a fertile model for the future.

I cannot envisage a more exciting model than that developed by the band of 40 (a magic number historically) of rebel GPs who met in Telford on a grey Saturday morning. Locality commissioning meets all the desired elements in a system which will herald a new dawn of co-operation, commitment and goodwill between health professionals, managers and – most important of all – the patients whom we serve. Such a vision, clothed in mechanisms which can be tried and tested can, and I believe will, transform despair first into hope, then into confidence and enthusiasm.

I commend this book with much pleasure.

SANDY MACARA
October 1997

Foreword

A matter of commonsense may still take time to become accepted common knowledge. The need for commissioning within the health service is one such case. It provides another example of how some of the most fundamentally important changes in the NHS have arisen from within general practice. Other great landmarks include the formation of the Royal College in 1952, the Charter for the Family Doctor Service in 1964, and the development of practice-based computer systems in the late 1970s and early 1980s. Contrary to the views of many politicians, general practice is a fertile seedbed for innovation at a fundamental level. It should be encouraged rather than stifled, for it is difficult to think of original contributions from governments of equal standing to those mentioned above.

In 1989 the government of the day made a cardinal error in its plans to reform the NHS. It assumed that any GPs who wanted to become involved in developing their local health services would also want to become purchasers of secondary care. While introducing a split between purchaser and provider it ignored the difference between commissioning and purchasing. Indeed, it ignored the need to involve all relevant bodies in the coordinated planning and review of local services and preferred to advocate the opposite – a market economy in which GPs who became purchasers were advantaged over those who did not, and in which different practices were in effect encouraged to break up the goals of cohesion and equity within local services. Morale within both primary and secondary care plummeted.

It took general practice itself to respond to these damaging policies. From 1990 on, groups of GPs around the country thought things out for themselves and in a significant number of cases received considerable help from their health authorities and local hospitals. Their work showed a remarkable uniformity. They wanted to help plan local services and ensure that their plans achieved the intended results, but they had professional and personal misgivings about becoming direct purchasers of secondary care, particularly at a practice level. Nonetheless theirs was a fragmented movement operating in a politically hostile environment. It was not until late 1994 that these small specks of mercury coalesced into a single whole, large enough to be seen and harness the enthusiasm and commitment of GPs to influence national policies.

While progress was made in influencing the Conservative government there remained an ideological conflict that hindered progress which may never have been truly overcome. It was the incoming Labour government of 1997 that was more in tune with the concept of commissioning – it is thus a result of the 1997 election that commissioning moved in three years from anarchy to government policy. What is required now is for politicians, civil servants, managers and clinicians to make it work; to develop an efficient, effective, accountable service within which it is a pleasure to work.

That is what this book is about. It provides an excellent starting point for those new to commissioning whilst at the same time acting as a workshop manual for those already engaged in developing cohesive local services. I would be surprised if there is anyone in the country who cannot learn from it with benefit. It is the first handbook of commissioning and follows on naturally from the seminal work on the theoretical background to commissioning written by Ron Singer in early 1997. Other 'how to do it' books will follow of course but *The Locality Commissioning Handbook* will forever remain the first. I congratulate its authors on producing such a valuable book in such a timely manner.

ANDREW WILLIS
October 1997

About the authors

Michael Dixon is a full time GP in Cullompton, Devon. Prior to the 1990 reforms he was a member of the Exeter LMC and sat on the District Management Team and board of the then Exeter Health Authority. At the beginning of 1993 he co-founded the Mid-Devon Family Doctors Commissioning Group and remains its secretary. He is a member of the National Executive of the National Association of Commissioning GPs and an Honorary Research Fellow at Exeter University.

Topsy Murray has a background in the voluntary sector and was chair of the Exeter Community Health Council between 1986 and 1990. Since then she has worked for the North & East Devon Health Authority and is Locality Co-Ordinator for Mid-Devon.

David Jenner is also a full time GP in Cullompton, Devon and was co-founder of the Mid-Devon Family Doctors Commissioning Group. He is chairman of the group and also the Locality Medical Director for Mid-Devon employed by the North & East Devon Health Authority.

List of contributors

Liz Cosford
Team Manager, Primary Care Audit Group
North & East Devon Health
Dean Clarke House
Southernhay East
Exeter
Devon EX1 1PQ

Mark Couldrick
General Practitioner
The Surgery
Station Road
Hemyock
Devon EX15 3SF

Jeremy Hallett
Chief Executive
Wiltshire Health Authority
Southgate House
Pans Lane
Devizes
Wiltshire SN10 5EQ

Stephen Henry
Past Chairman of the NACGP
Maidens Cottage
Bapton
Warminster
Wiltshire BA12 0SD

John Jacob
Consultant Surgeon
West of England Eye Unit
Royal Devon and Exeter Hospital (Wonford)
Barrack Road
Exeter
Devon EX2 5DW

Terry Jones
Community Health Council Member
Venbridge Barn
Cheriton Bishop
Devon EX6 6HD

Steve Jupp
Director of Acute Hospital Trust
Royal Devon and Exeter Hospital (Wonford)
Barrack Road
Exeter
Devon EX2 5DW

Richard Leete
General Practitioner
Wyndham House Surgery
Silverton
Devon EX5 4HZ

Donald McLintock
Clinical Research Fellow
The Surgery
Station Road
Hemyock
Devon EX15 3SF

Virginia Pearson
Consultant in Public Health
North & East Devon Health
Dean Clarke House
Southernhay East
Exeter
Devon EX1 1PQ

Acknowledgements

This book is the collective work of many but no one is to blame for the views put forward apart from the editors. First and foremost this book should acknowledge the work of all those who have made personal sacrifices in the name of GP commissioning. Particular thanks for the help of all those on the Executive of the National Association of Commissioning GPs (NACGPs) though once again this book should not be seen as representing either their own individual or collective views of the NACGP. Andrew Willis for his positive criticism and good advice and Alan Birchall for providing information and input to the chapter on commissioning structures. Chaand Nagpaul for his help on the role of LMCs and pharmaceutical firms and Ron Singer for the inspiration provided by his own book – *GP Commissioning: an inevitable evolution*. Also Stephen Cushing, Jonathan Shapiro, Keith Edgar, William Warin and Martin Shaw. Thanks too to GPs and managers from other groups who provided input – John Doherty, Ashok Vora, Peter Bailey, Sarb Gidda and Pat Jones. Thanks also to the local pioneers who developed our model of commissioning in Mid-Devon, particularly members of the group Executive – Hugh Savill, Jonathan Stead, Charles Kent and Tom Bell. Also, Clare Landymore, the first practice manager to sit on the Mid-Devon Executive. Also to Jeremy Hallett (Chief Executive, Wiltshire Health Authority) and to the health authority executives and managers who encouraged and supported us – Trevor Bailey, Peter Jackson, Gillian Morgan and John Bewick. More locally still, thanks to all the partners and staff at my own practice, College Surgery, Cullompton, for all their tolerance and kindness. Across the Atlantic thanks to Drs David and Christine Hibbard for providing an American perspective.

Closer to home I owe much to Joanna, my wife, for telling me to stop moaning and do something. She has fully supported my efforts in GP commissioning and in writing this book and has been a pillar of support, common sense and humour. My children, Finn, May and Liberty have been more than patient with my physical and mental absences in recent months. Also my brother Andrew, who died at the end of April 1997, a few days before the project began. His courage and selflessness provided a driving inspiration.

Finally to the three people most involved in this project. Topsy Murray, our Locality Manager in Mid-Devon, who contributed to Chapter 3 and a large part of Chapters 6 and 9. She provided a much needed health authority perspective, not to mention a first class brain and a lot of sense. Many of the ideas in this book originated from conversations and heated debates with her and David Jenner, who is also our Locality Medical Director as well as Chairman and co-founder of the Mid-Devon Commissioning Group. Last, but not least, I owe everything to Christine Quinn, who has ever efficiently transcribed the whole book from the first scribbled note to the final manuscript. She has an uncanny ability to read minds as well as being able to translate tapes with backgrounds that varied from cars, trains and aeroplanes to seagulls at St Ives and the Teletubbies.

Many of those concerned have become friends, all the good bits in this book are a result of their work and the excellent contributors whom I also thank.

MICHAEL DIXON
October 1997

To Jana

Introduction

At first it was 'GP commissioning'. Its arrival was announced in the Spring of 1994 by a band of 40 rebel GPs who had met in Telford on a grey Saturday morning. Later it was to be called 'locality commissioning' but the names remain interchangeable. Whatever we call it, it has rapidly spread to include almost 50% of patients, GPs and health authorities in one form or another in only three years. Its successful formula is that of a popular grass roots movement pitting common sense against central dogma and this is what now makes GP commissioning unstoppable. Although practical and financial support has been slow to come from the centre, the ideological argument has already been won among most non-fundholders, fundholders and health managers. Officially at least, GP commissioning is now the preferred model and it is up to GP commissioners to deliver the goods.

A handbook on GP commissioning is long overdue. In a way it is a contradiction in terms because, at present, there are no fixed rules on how it should be done, with very few 'do's' and 'don'ts'. It is therefore up to every group to find its own path. Indeed the excitement of GP commissioning is that it is truly a 'tabula rasa' upon which every GP, manager and patient can make his mark. A book that is prescriptive or didactic would be out of place. The main purpose of this book is simply to enable and inspire GPs, health professionals and other managers to establish their own vision of the NHS in their locality. We hope that it will be a guide to the sort of questions that any GP commissioning group will need to answer and provide the format that those answers might take. A secondary purpose of the book is to explain to others exactly what GP commissioners are trying to do.

The only qualification of the authors is that they have been involved in GP commissioning for some years and therefore know some of the pitfalls and most of the questions. The book also incorporates many of the lessons learnt by other commissioning groups along with their successes and failures and it is therefore, in a sense, the collective work of all those who have been involved in GP commissioning to date. There is, perhaps, only one fixed rule for GP commissioning – that it should commission services which are appropriate for that locality, appropriate for its GPs, population (taking into account both wishes and needs), demography, social structure, cultural history and available resources. The structure and function of any group should therefore be largely a function of what the GPs, other health professionals, managers and the local population think that it should be. Their aim should be to provide the most cost-effective care for the people of that locality given the resources available and to do this in a spirit of co-operation where everyone can be involved. Anything else is not GP commissioning.

It was one of the governing principles of this book that it should be written only by those who are actively involved in the GP commissioning process. This includes the GPs themselves (fundholders and non-fundholders), practice managers, consultants, locality managers, a trust manager, a Chief Executive of a district health authority, a public health consultant, a primary care audit manager and a patient. All are stakeholders in the locality commissioning process. They provide a vision of a 'bottom-up NHS', which is ruled not by diktat but by co-operation and partnership between them all. GP commissioning was a reaction to the frustration of many GPs, who felt that the NHS centre had become out of touch and had ceased to listen to them. They had become demoralized by the unworkable schemes that had been imposed on them and the general attitude of 'mother knows best'. There was also a lack of vision and an assumption that the religion of cost efficiency had to exclude co-operation, equity, goodwill and commitment. This frustration gave way to action but GPs must continue to keep ownership of their movement if it is to succeed and thrive. That is why all GPs should become involved in GP commissioning in some way or other and why they should be involved in developing and adapting the model to suit their local requirements. It is the sort of collective opportunity that general practice has never had before and if we fail to seize it now it may not come again.

Chapter 1 begins with a definition of GP/locality commissioning and explains why it matters and what it offers GPs and patients. It may come as no surprise that the contributing fundholder, non-fundholder, health authority chief executive and patient all come to similar conclusions. What is interesting is the way in which they come to that same conclusion from very different perspectives using different arguments and even different languages. In Chapter 2 we offer ten principles, which have increasingly emerged as the important elements in GP commissioning. Chapter 3 represents both a GP and a health authority view on how to get a GP commissioning group started. Its pace may seem a bit pedestrian for the fully developed GP commissioning group but it is designed to help those who are trying to get up and running by focusing on the very different perspectives of GPs and health authority managers when they enter this process. Chapter 4 looks at the possible structures that a GP commissioning group might have and the function of different elements within each structure. The structures of various existing GP commissioning groups are analysed though space inevitably means that many excellent and dynamic groups had to be omitted.

The next four chapters look at the role of locality commissioning groups in each of the four stages of the commissioning cycle. In Chapter 5 Virginia Pearson looks at the first element in this cycle – 'How are we to assess the needs of a locality?' If we are to establish a health service based upon needs then this has to be the first task of any locality commissioning group. She asks how we might manage and meet such needs and how public health at district level can be made relevant to, and become devolved to, locality groups. Her example shows how this might work in practice.

In Chapter 6 we look at the prime task of GP commissioning – planning. One of the main tasks of a GP commissioning group will be to write a locality health strategy and this chapter shows how groups can do this. It reviews the planning cycle, and use of information available at practice, locality and national level and how to develop action plans and medium-term strategies based upon it. The chapter focuses on how all local health related services can be integrated within a locality health strategy and how, outside the locality, the plans of a GP commissioning group must be integrated with those at district level and also with the plans of local trusts.

Though commissioning and purchasing are quite distinct, some commissioning groups have been variously involved in purchasing as a means of seeing that their plans are followed through. Chapter 7 looks at how GP commissioning groups can be involved in strategic purchasing decisions. The essence of such involvement is that it is a co-operative one with the local district health authority where the latter holds the final authority and remains financially accountable. Furthermore, any changes brought about in trust performance are available to all patients, GPs and locality commissioning groups. The chapter looks at purchasing new services, improving services already purchased from a local trust, how to get more for your money and how money can be transferred between different secondary services and between secondary and primary services. The chapter examines the reactions of a consultant and a trust manager who have been through the procedure, as purchasing 'locality commissioning style' is a collaborative process. It ends with thorny questions such as the holding of budgets, the purchasing of primary care and joint purchasing with others such as social services.

In Chapter 8 we look at the final stage of the commissioning cycle – assessment and audit. GP commissioning groups need to audit their work in order to see if they have obtained appropriate services for their patients. Increasingly, the trust and goodwill within groups is such that they are able to start auditing the standards of care within their member practices as well. The chapter also looks at the way that commissioning groups, and GPs within them, will need to develop their use of evidence in making rational commissioning decisions and also in the individual care of their patients. It ends by considering the importance of information technology and the resources that groups will need for it.

Chapter 9 looks at the issue of accountability in locality commissioning. First, how can GP commissioning groups make themselves accountable to the local population and draw up a structure for doing this? Second, how can groups become accountable to health authorities and the Department of Health in terms of both financial accountability and the taking on of central strategies? This chapter also explores the concept of clinical accountability and looks at how GP commissioning groups can begin to involve other professionals in the process. Chapter 10 describes the GP commissioning pilots and the locality prescribing budgets that go with them. It also looks at where the pharmaceutical industry might fit into a future commissioning model.

Finally in Chapter 11, the editors allow themselves a leap of imagination in looking towards the future. What will future locality commissioning groups look like and what will be their relationships with each other, district health authorities, trusts and the Department of Health? To what extent will commissioning groups be involved in improving and setting the standards in primary care and developing research? Will they be landed with a rationing role and what resources will they require for any of these roles? The chapter ends with a vision of where locality commissioning might lead.

Those involved in GP commissioning so far have been enthusiasts and their enthusiasm and motivation may have been largely responsible for its success. The challenge over the next few years will be to show that the model itself is robust, effective and can be generalized. GPs are now war-weary with change and it is understandable they should doubt that further tinkering with the mechanism of the NHS will make any difference. Is it simply a case of taking on ever more responsibility with ever decreasing thanks and remuneration? Fundholders may question whether locality commissioning can be as decisive and effective in its purchasing role as many fundholders feel that they have been. They may be concerned that a surfeit of consensus and co-operation may slow things down. They will hopefully be reassured by the possibilities of being involved in purchasing decisions and by the realization that planning is not only a primary but also a far more fundamental and important way of changing the way that services are provided. They may also be relieved to join a system where equity and fairness come first. Nevertheless, the answer for both fund-holders and non-fundholders is that they must create a model that works for them all. The difference between this and previous models, which have been handed down from above, is that GPs can all be involved together and for the first time they are in a position to make serious commissioning decisions. There are some who doubt whether GPs can rise to the occasion and sign up to such a policy of co-operation – GP commissioners believe that they can. Indeed if any GP questions whether he or she should be doing this then he or she must be prepared to answer one question – 'Who else would you like to do it for you?'

We hope that this book will act as a focus of debate for those who want to make the GP commissioning process work. The NHS may be about to see a new dawn of professional co-operation, commitment and goodwill. Part of that goodwill may be the trust given to GPs in letting them evolve their own systems for commissioning care locally. GPs, for their own part, will need to show the NHS that they are both motivated and able to do the job. If they are and if they can then general practice will be able to take the credit for inventing and developing a system that will propel a fairer and more cost-effective NHS into the 21st Century.

1 What is locality commissioning?

Introduction

Locality commissioning means, quite literally, empowering the locality to obtain health services that are appropriate for the local population. It is synonymous with the term GP commissioning which emphasizes the central role of locality GPs in ensuring that the locality gets the services that it needs and desires. It represents a shift in strategic control from the district health authority (DHA) to the locality GPs though in most models the DHA retains operational control in planning and purchasing local services.

The 'locality' part of locality commissioning thus distinguishes it from 'district wide' commissioning by the DHA and from 'practice-based' purchasing by fundholders (which is not really commissioning anyway). It does not preclude commissioning at district level for those services which are more appropriately purchased and planned centrally, and nor does it preclude fundholding at practice level as historically many fundholders have also been locality commissioners.

The 'commissioning' part of locality commissioning incorporates a broad concept and can involve all the processes from assessing the need for health care, through its planning, specification and purchasing, to the monitoring of performance and evaluation of outcome. The National Association of Commissioning GPs (NACGP) has defined commissioning as 'the process of gathering and analysing the wants and needs of a population, and identifying the services required to meet those needs' (*see* Appendix 1). Commissioning plans are strategic and free of resource consideration but do involve the setting of priorities. Nevertheless, this makes commissioning a quite distinct activity from purchasing which is defined by the NACGP as 'the interpretation of commissioning plans, and the construction and implementation of time-related purchasing plans'. This clearly does not exclude commissioning groups from becoming involved in purchasing but establishes it as a secondary role in which the DHA remains both final authority and financial arbiter. It is their prime involvement in planning decisions that distinguishes such groups from other models such as total purchasing projects and multi-funds.

Locality commissioning groups go about their work in a number of different ways within a variety of structures as we shall see (*see* Chapter 4). They are involved in making planning decisions both at locality and district level in conjunction with their local health authority and in the needs assessment which precedes such decisions. Some are beginning to develop local locality health strategies, which incorporate all health-related agencies at locality level and ensure that the resulting plans and services provided are integrated with other agencies such as social services. Many groups, with the support of their DHA, have developed public health and needs assessment to locality level and are also increasingly involved in auditing both their commissioning performance and the services provided within the locality. Their involvement in purchasing is confined to strategic decisions and is subsidiary to their main commissioning role. Some are involved in an advisory purchasing role to their DHA. Others are more directly involved in purchasing decisions either by representation on a health authority purchasing board or by close involvement with locality management teams devolved from the DHA.

In the midst of such diversity, a generic model of locality commissioning is beginning to appear which lays emphasis on GP leadership and a close relationship with the local DHA.

Geographical definition

The geographical definition of a locality commissioning group (LCG) is simply that it should cover the whole population of that locality and all its GPs. The boundaries of the first localities were decided by the GPs themselves but these are increasingly being decided either by DHAs or more commonly by DHAs and GPs in conjunction. The size of localities originally foreseen by the present government were between 50 000 and 150 000 patients although many locality commissioning groups are several times this size. All that matters is that LCGs in total represent the same population as the health authority. Ron Singer has suggested that medium-sized commissioning groups may be appropriate for rural and semi-rural areas while larger commissioning groups will be required for inner cities where they may need to deal with several trusts.[1] This point is taken up in Chapter 6 when we look at the problem of how to co-ordinate the plans of localities and local trusts.

Unlike some of the total purchasing projects, locality commissioning groups cover a whole area rather than a group of interested GPs and, therefore, the GPs are bound to be variously committed, interested or even apathetic towards the locality commissioning process. One of the most important aspects of locality commissioning is that all GPs within the locality are potentially included and invited into the group. As with any group of this sort, there will be a few doing most of the work, a larger number supporting them and the majority happy for them to dictate the pace provided they have a veto when they are unhappy. As an all-inclusive process locality commissioning would ideally proceed with total consensus but in the real world there are bound to be occasions when it has to proceed according to the majority decision of its locality GPs. This concept of a majority vote may be very foreign to GPs who by tradition are fiercely individual, but the alternative is for locality GPs to give up their say on what sort of locality services they are going to have and pass the decision-making to someone else.

It represents a major change from the situation prior to 1990, when health decisions and health provision were organized centrally by the DHA and GP input to this decision making was minimal. As localities become the focus of commissioning activity, health authorities are having to learn to devolve control to their locality GPs at the same time as the GPs themselves are having to learn to abide by corporate decisions. Not surprisingly, for some health authorities, and even a few GPs, this has been almost one step too far within a culture of continuous change.

Definition by function

The main function of locality commissioning is concerned with *planning* local services. At this level they can provide a short- and long-term perspective on which locality services are required. In so doing, they are able to take in the perspective of all other health related services, e.g. social services, housing, education and probation, and thus produce a fully integrated locality health strategy. This can also take into account the further perspectives of the health authority, local trusts and central priorities within the NHS. The result is a far more cohesive, integrated and forward looking approach than that which can be offered by purchasing alone.

Their co-operative involvement with health authorities in strategic *purchasing* does nevertheless complement this planning role as a means of answering the 'how' as well as the 'what' questions. It also provides them with potential access to 100%, rather than the fundholders' 30%, of purchasing decisions without the need to accept the encumbrances of budgetary responsibility. Their greatest involvement so far has been in catalysing health authorities to purchase new services required by local GPs and improving services provided by local trusts. They have only occasionally been instrumental in switching a contract for a given service from one trust to another (*see* Chapter 7). Some are now working towards a co-operative role with their DHA in deciding how money is allocated and spent in the belief that this will make them more effective commissioners. This may, in theory, give them a greater ability to vire resources and change services but it will also involve them in difficult decisions such as where to cut (or in NHS vernacular 'disinvest') services, which ones are less necessary and where and how money for one service can be saved and removed for use in contracting for a more needed service. Such involvement, nevertheless, needs to remain entirely optional with no personal financial consequences to GPs who do or do not take on such a role.

LCGs are also beginning to take on a greater responsibility at the beginning and end of what is known as the commissioning cycle (*see* Figure 1.1).

Needs assessment, traditionally the domain of public health, is becoming increasingly locality specific thereby enabling LCGs to plan locality specific services to meet those needs. At the end of the commissioning cycle locality commissioning groups are developing an increasing role in auditing and evaluating services in order to see if their commissioning decisions have met the needs and targets that they were supposed to. Many have taken on a supportive role for general practitioners in their locality, often in parallel with their LMC and local primary care audit group which has allowed them to become involved in audit, education and

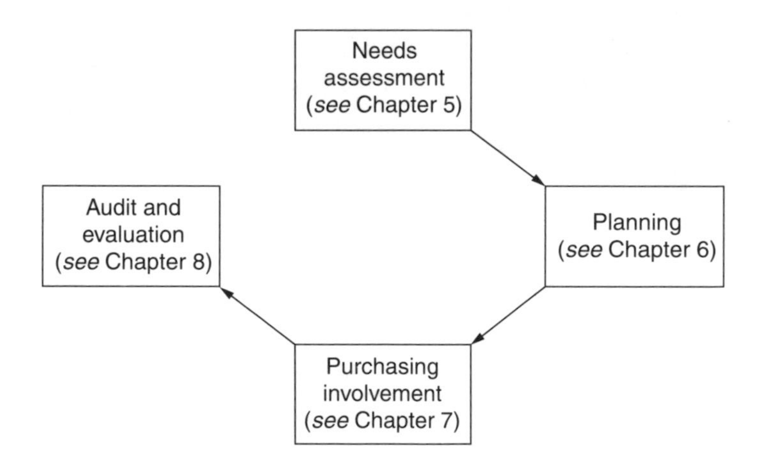

Figure 1.1: Functions of a locality commissioning group.

evidence-based medicine. Some are working to raise the standards of general practice within their locality. Intervention of this sort might be very threatening to GPs if it came from an outside agency but it appears to be much less so within the context of a locality commissioning group. To quote William Warin, NACGP Executive member and non-fundholder, 'by virtue of GPs working in a similar way to similar standards and to similar protocols, GPs actually feel supported and helped rather than beleaguered'.

Historical perspective: locality commissioning/ GP commissioning – what is the difference?

In the beginning there was just GP commissioning. These groups evolved shortly after the introduction of the purchaser/provider split and fundholding and usually comprised non-fundholding GPs who did not want to become fundholders but who were keen to make sure that their patients did not lose out in the 'new NHS'. They were GP led and their effectiveness largely depended upon whether the local DHA was sympathetic or not. Progressive DHAs soon recognized their importance and some gave financial support and adapted their own structures to make the best possible use of the work of these groups.

Many fundholders joined and were welcomed into the groups as they too saw the advantages of being potentially involved in 100% rather than 30% of purchasing decisions and in taking on a far more crucial planning role. They also began to enjoy the feeling of companionship and consensus engendered by working together with all GPs in a locality. Where such groups had not spontaneously formed in this way, other DHAs saw the advantages and some divided their districts into localities and became themselves pro-active in setting up locality groups. These locality groups had exactly the same function as the GP commissioning groups that preceded them but 'GP commissioning' began to change its label to 'locality commissioning'. Many health authorities felt uneasy at the rapid devolvement of many of their previous roles to GPs in the localities and may have felt easier with the term 'locality commissioning'. Health economists and politicians also seemed to prefer the term. In the end it is simply a case of 'a rose by any other name'. If we call it 'locality commissioning' or 'GP commissioning' it will remain a concept invented by GPs themselves and one which will rely for the foreseeable future on having GPs in partnership with health authorities at the helm. Undoubtedly other groups of managers and professionals will become closely involved as time goes by but this may be appropriate only when these groups have established effective long-term working relationships with member GPs, the health authority and local providers. If 'GP commissioning' is to be called 'locality commissioning' (as it will be mostly for the remainder of this book) then it may remove GPs from the firing line but for the time being they are likely to remain in the driving seat as the main cog in a primary care-led NHS.

What does locality commissioning offer GPs and patients?

Locality commissioning provides an equitable system where all GPs and patients within a locality are included and where each GP can be as little or as much involved as he wishes to be. For GPs overall this means maximum empowerment with minimum absence from their surgeries. Furthermore, the ability to be advocates for their patients in the locality in the role of commissioner still allows them to retain individual advocacy for each patient as a GP in the surgery. Keith Edgar, NACGP Executive member and fundholding GP, puts it thus, 'GPs can only master the paradox of providing individual advocacy while ensuring justice for the wider population within democratic and transparent commissioning structures'. In locality commissioning, unlike fundholding, GPs are not compromised by having any financial interest in how they use the money that has been earmarked for their patients. Indeed in locality commissioning the money for patient care should go much further as the economies of scale would dictate that commissioning at locality, rather than practice, level is likely to minimize overall management and information technology costs.

Some of the strengths of locality commissioning amount to unforeseen by-products. The closer links between GPs and their practices are leading to a common commitment to improve and develop general practice within the localities. The closer links with consultants are also leading to a fertile exchange of ideas and a common vision, which can only lead to better co-ordination of primary and secondary care and the interface between them.

Locality commissioning, however, offers different things to different people depending upon their perspective.

A non-fundholder's view

Richard Leete

History

Our practice felt most vulnerable when the government of the day came up with the idea of 'fundholding'. Like many in our locality we were small and rural. Surely it would mean the 'big city boys' buying all the decent surgeons and squeezing us out? In a spirit of self defence we decided to fight back. We explored the possibility of a consortium of three rural practices and took part in the preparatory year for the first wave of fundholding. In the end our practice got 'cold feet'. Ideologically we felt unhappy as part of a gigantic ploy to favour one part of general practice at the expense of the rest. Answers to our questions were always met by reassurance and it was clear that the region was writing the rules as it went along. We left the other two to continue the consortium on its own and were only too pleased when our absence did not affect them.

It was quite a relief to find that most of the general practitioners around us had also decided to stay out of the scheme and with excellent local secondary care the impact also seemed less dramatic than first feared. We were approached by a local town practice to join a 'non-fundholder group' which most of the GPs in the middle of the country joined. We were pleased to be 100% non-fundholding. We already knew each other well as there had been an educational forum of the same GPs for some years. We felt supported.

The group seemed to develop quite quickly. There was a sense of common identity which transcended the sometimes vociferous discussions. We realized that our practices cared for perhaps 25% of the catchment area of our local district general hospital (DGH) and we began to wonder if perhaps we had some clout after all. We were told that if we were to withdraw our block contract it could ruin a whole department. It would take an extra year of notice over the fundholders but it could be done. So we did have power after all. Things were looking up. At the same time we had little desire to threaten consultants we knew and respected. Perhaps the way forward was to work with the consultants to develop referral criteria which would avoid any need to withdraw contracts. It was the first start towards a link between clinicians to plan care across the primary/secondary interface. At times there was an impression that we made both purchaser and provider management uncomfortable. There was an additional bonus of understanding and education. This was most apparent, for example, in drawing up criteria for a fast-track knee service. The end result contained elements of both social as well as clinical need.

The clinical forum continued. Consultants were keen to discuss their interests and the ways in which GPs could use their skills most efficiently. It still felt like a clinical pressure group. A proposal to have practice managers on the group executive was at this stage rejected. Much bitterness was felt about the financial advantage to fundholding, especially for IT costs. To us, fundholding was prepared to hold a threat against the main providers whilst, on the other hand, the non-fundholding group was following a path of collaboration in these early days. The local papers did not always seem to get this spirit across but the good communication between clinicians prevented any major stress. In common with fundholders our group was having a real input to management strategy.

Locality

The evidence of a two-tier system, or three tiers if one includes private practice, was all too plain to see. The local fundholders were largely reluctant but realistic and keen to get the best for their patients. There were murmurings in our group of going towards a gigantic fundholder status to protect ourselves. Those of us who had computers were spending money just trying to keep up with fundholders, some of whom had never before been computerized but who now had fully funded systems worth many thousands of pounds.

With the merger of the FHSA and HA into a new health authority came the idea of splitting the country into localities. Our group formed a majority component of one such locality. The new health authority was supportive and the concept seemed to strengthen our group identity. Other practices in the locality had expressed a wish to join and these included fundholding units. Perhaps surprisingly there was no opposition to including fundholders who were welcomed in. It seemed that the division between colleagues was overstated and this was one way to achieve progress.

As we now move towards locality purchasing, these original principles prevail. We have the benefit of having built a strong relationship between individual GPs. This is built on a keenness to share clinical information, support each other and get the best care for our patients. We have learnt enough to realize that resources are limited and that we can greatly influence how the money is spent. There is tremendous benefit in having the purchaser/provider management split linked to a collaborative relationship between clinicians on both sides. This creates an independent third arm to the management triangle.

Leadership

The steady development of the group's identity and functions has been greatly helped by the enthusiasm of the health authority and those GPs prepared to give time to the executive group. The ordinary GP has been able to keep in touch over pizza and beer once a quarter. Most practices manage a representative at every such meeting which confirms the extent of support for the group's work.

The keystone of primary care has always been the independent contractor status. Fear of government intervention and manipulation pushed many into fundholding, believing this was the only way to preserve their autonomy. It led to a massive increase in administrative procedures, often taking a GP away from clinical work to front the management. It seemed the motivation for these practice-based activities was inward looking and factional. Our group was having to look out to fellow practices, the health authority itself and the trusts to keep its presence felt. A powerful leadership group was even looking out to other similar groups elsewhere in the country and was becoming well known. It felt right. The extraordinary feeling has been that individual practices have been able to carry on business as usual. Of course the battle for resources, the poor pay awards and increased patient expectation have taken their toll on morale but the fear that we might become the Cinderella of general practice has not been realized.

The future of formalized locality commissioning with a budget and a level playing field with fundholding is the logical extension of our current group status. For a small practice like ours, it is an attractive proposition. We have already debated many issues within the membership and the relationships have strengthened. Tentative discussions about moving resources from one area to another have met with far less opposition than if proposed by the health authority itself. Savings on extra-contractual referrals have provided local hospital beds, which in turn have been cost-efficient on DGH usage. Suspicion has given way to realism. So is everything perfect in this imperfect world? What are the challenges ahead? The leadership needs to continue its enthusiasm and independence from the health authority. It needs to be trusted and seen as one of us. There must be no feeling of being manipulated into making the 'right' decisions and it needs to represent the views of both individual members and the group itself. The backing of a properly elected executive group is vital. The pool of GPs to provide this expertise is over 60 which is big enough to provide a turnover of leadership if this is ever felt necessary and small enough to keep in touch with individual practices.

The future

Tough decisions lie ahead. Our membership includes small towns and scattered rural communities. Geography will influence priorities. Inevitably there will be occasions when one member's view will have to give way to that of the majority. Already this is seen in a small way when, for example, a particular member's concern, such as community psychiatric nurse (CPN) input to practices, is pushed off the agenda because of lack of time. At a member's forum recently a suggestion was made to create an independent arbitration process, a kind of ombudsman for any practice to access in the event of real grievance.

I have not mentioned the wider concepts of commissioning like the difficult collaboration which lies ahead involving decisions over prescribing from an agreed formulary or sharing resources for nursing care. There are also challenges in the future involving the integration of health and social services and needs assessment surveys of our locality.

Progress towards more influence over our future must continue at a measured pace. The exchange of information and development of common protocols of care, particularly in the clinical arena, have been a bonus. We have done several group audits and we now look towards evidence-based medicine to back our strategies. Such controversial concepts would have been unthinkable to many of us a few years ago. Nevertheless, they are happening in the group. The reason for this is the sense of common purpose, realism and an optimal group size; big enough to be radical and adapt to change but small enough for all of us to retain our individual identity. It is this formula of size that underpins the great potential of locality commissioning.

A fundholder's view

The National Association of Commissioning GPs has always been committed to bridging the divide between fundholders and non-fundholders. Quite spontaneously, fundholders are beginning to see locality commissioning as a more developed version of many of the things that fundholding seemed to offer. Dr Nigel Sylvester, fundholder and chairman of the Mid-Hampshire Commissioning Group, writes 'As a first wave fundholder, I acknowledge the benefits that the health reforms have brought. However, the system has now reached its full potential and it is time to move on. Locality commissioning offers the advantage of the purchaser/provider split without the huge costs of individual patient invoicing, annual contracts, fragmented strategic planning and the undeniable two-tier service. Those at the cutting edge have nothing to fear'. His views are echoed by Dr Stephen Henry who presents a representative view of those who have been at the sharp end of fundholding since its inception.

Stephen Henry

There is no doubt that fundholding has proved catalytic and innovative at practice level. Through the power of the cheque book one or two 'partners', GP or fund manager, can make the decision and deliver the service for their patients as individuals, and not just make the case and hope someone else does something about it. This has changed the balance of influence between hospitals and the community; something that health authorities have been unable to do in 50 years.

In 1991, the preparatory year for first wavers, it did not take long to realize that 'to make something happen' reaching critical mass is required for significant change. To reach it you have to work in partnership – collaboration not confrontation. Fundholders had to work with fellow GPs to arrange community facilities like outpatients and local diagnostics fairly; with trusts to close a ward, downsize a department or re-engineer a service; and with health authorities to share purchasing experiences for the population with that of the individual.

By 1992, fundholders were lobbying the Secretary of State for a practice-based contract rather than the present doctor-based one because if offered all the staff, such as nurses and managers, an equal stake in the business. It was a contract to deliver total care by commissioning that primary care could not provide itself, to set national, locally adjusted targets and standards, i.e. fundholding within a commissioned framework. Hence the total purchasing pilots. Four became 80 by popular demand with some 300 practices attempting to balance the uncontrollable acute sector against the predictable elective and, anathema to bona-fide commissioners, within a fixed budget. These are in effect self-selected commissioning groups but not necessarily of coterminous practices and mostly without non-fundholders. Total purchasing stepped up coterminous practices and mostly without non-fundholders. Total purchasing stepped up the necessity for partnerships to a new level through genuine involvement in strategic planning and an overwhelming need for public health support and risk sharing within the health authority.

We have moved on from the historical focus on the consultation between doctor and patient being the be-all and end-all of general practice, although it remains the cornerstone, through the 'doctor, his patient, the illness' to encompass 'the practice, its patients, their health' towards starting to address 'the locality, the authorities (health and social), their contract'.

As foreshadowed in *Primary Care: The Future*, the aims are:

- commissioning, preferably by all round agreement, for outcomes and not just activity: are patients better as a result of treatment and does it represent value for money?
- increasing consumer influence and community involvement: what does the patient want?
- accountability: for appropriate prescribing, appropriate referrals, the use of a fair share of resources and a comprehensive range of services.

So the approach to operational strategy is two-fold. What is appropriate in terms of place, time and personnel? What is the skill-mix required? A multi-disciplinary multi-professional approach to the second strand, to deliver and control services and not just 'pass the parcel' across the old institutional boundaries in the search for seamlessness.

In 1997, fundholding is at a stage where for most the figures are now robust enough to go for economies of scale and revert to block agreements instead of cost per case contracts, sharing information and relying on each other. It could not have happened without the experience and data collection of fundholding which was a means to an end. So fundholders are already logically moving into locality groups large enough to tackle acute and elective services appropriately but still with the individual patient as the base line. It is not a return to health authority population purchasing.

But there were always shortcomings to the scheme as it was originally implemented. Although fundholding was voluntary, the incentives themselves were divisive – management allowances, computers and savings being seen as lining doctor's pockets, souring the relationships between those GPs for and against. The cost of transactions and incentives was high and there was a potential conflict of interest between financial considerations and clinical judgements. There could be confrontation with hospital trusts and a sense of loss of power by consultants. For health authorities, stung by the trojan horse of successful fundholder purchasing, there was fragmentation of strategic planning.

There were outside perceptions of inequity and media championing of a two-tier system. From the GPs' point of view, there was no take-home pay for the extra work downloaded from hospitals due to the barriers between funding streams and the inability to get money back out of existing hospital contracts (as it reduces their inviolable quantum) or at marginal costs only, hamstringing primary care development.

The advantage of locality commissioning is that it can offer the whole local community, however defined, all the advantages now held by the total purchasing practices without a health authority or trust being able to divide and rule. For fundholders it removes the stigmata and eliminates the shortcomings. The differences between 'grown-up' fundholding and commissioning are now a matter of semantics. If the historical baggage of mutual distrust can be laid aside in the light of common aims expressed by fundholding and commissioning organizations, then the divergent poles of general practice can coalesce to address the issues each side has left out of the equation. For the commissioners, what to do about resource allocation and accountability for a limited budget, and for fundholders the greatest good for the greatest number at the expense of the advantages to their individual patients and practices.

A health authority's view

Jeremy Hallett

If chaos theory confirms that a butterfly can have significant impact on the world's weather systems by flapping its wings, then surely in similar fashion we can influence events beyond our day-to-day experience. Locality commissioning offers such a vehicle for fundamental change that will have similar significant traumatic impact which, if properly understood and managed, will take the NHS safely into the 21st Century, on course to maintain and improve the health of the people of the United Kingdom.

The UK stands out from most developed countries in the unique role of the GP, who is personally committed to total care for individuals. The challenge must be to build on this model and see health authorities move from planning and purchasing health services with GP support, to GPs moving 'centre stage' and planning and purchasing health care with health authority support. The advantages of such a system are impressive and will enable the development of a primary care-based health care system that supports the individual and allows them to remain in their home, or as close to their home as possible in order to maintain and improve their health.

The strategic thrust of locality commissioning must be to empower the primary care team – a team of multi-agency and disciplined professionals who, under the co-ordination of the general practice focus, will plan and purchase health care for their patients, working in conjunction with other primary care teams within a locality to provide co-ordinated and integrated health and social care. Locality commissioning will also encourage the GP to talk with the hospital clinician about decisions and choices, rather than 'grey suited individuals' brokering changes on behalf of the primary and secondary care clinicians.

Such a system, with its potential to focus accountability and responsibility at the lowest possible level in order to achieve sensible decisions, must bring with it clear managerial, financial and performance criteria. More importantly, there needs to exist a set of incentives that encourage GPs and other health care professionals to want to be involved and take on onerous responsibilities.

Key incentives are based on mutual respect between key players, financial rewards for good management, and the satisfaction of making something happen that benefits the public and the patient. All of this must be achieved within a relatively short time if we are to respond to the new health agenda which recognizes that the environment, education, social well being, jobs and self-respect have as much bearing on health as the maintenance of traditional forms of health services. Yet most time and expertise is concentrated on resolving the upsurge in emergency medical admissions and Patient Charter standards – an emphasis that reinforces a secondary care agenda. Health authorities must set an agenda that is about improving health and is focused and capable of delivering primary care-based services without being distracted by the heat of yesterday's fires.

The shift to primary care implies a corresponding change of emphasis in secondary care, not by stripping out resources to pay for primary care developments but rather by developing holistic models offering a continuum of support between home and hospital, with greater emphasis on the primary care model as the focus for the majority of health interventions.

The future of hospitals with their historical groupings of services will have to be reviewed – the downward pressure on resources, the impact of new technology, the challenge of clinical audit and effectiveness and the search for health outcome measurement. The Calman Hine report is the trojan horse of a fundamental rethink of the organization of high-tech resources to maximize clinical effectiveness.[2] Health authorities must see locality commissioning as an opportunity rather than a threat – a liberating opportunity that frees them up to 'hold the ring' to facilitate change and to move away from managing contracts to managing change.

Health authorities should provide leadership that demonstrates to the public and patient why changes are necessary, by setting and continually reviewing the agenda for health improvements and forging partnerships and alliances that bring about change. The health authority should become a strategic organization employing a few, highly skilled and competent individuals who focus on promoting good health, monitoring performance and encouraging best practice – a move towards a health assurance agency that is accountable for the priorities and choices that have to be made within service and financial frameworks, and ensuring through performance criteria that best practice and high quality services are provided.

The opportunity presents itself to achieve a true partnership, based on a mutual recognition of the respective contribution of general practice and the primary care team – to plan and manage local services – and the authority – to provide strategic leadership to manage change and facilitate and support locality commissioning.

If successful, locality commissioning will:

- be seen as the key way of engaging the public in considering how to maintain and improve their health and well being
- enable the health authority to 'hold the ring' in managing strategic change and assessing good health
- provide the framework for GP-led commissioning

- enable the involvement of the key agencies and organizations involved in the provision of health and social care
- facilitate joint planning with local authorities
- allow local plans to be developed that are based on health need and the views of local people.

The health authority will:

- hold the ring to facilitate change
- be the focus on quality
- provide specialist support
- be held publicly accountable
- be the focus for the health debate
- provide a strategic overview
- align people by listening and informing.

Finally, returning to chaos theory, none of this can happen without a change of mindset, particularly by the health authority. A new paradigm of health care planning and provision is required that empowers key individuals to bring about change to improve health, but within a strategic framework that encourages partnership, avoids confrontation and inspires people to take risks with suitable rewards in order to achieve the vision of empowered communities tackling ill health.

The debate about natural communities and the organization of locality commissioning must take place, but solutions should not be imposed from upon high. What must be established is the clear accountability for performance, with success factors and agreed monitoring arrangements. Resources for health care must be allocated to local commissioning teams and information systems must identify activity and costs that relate to primary care needs. Reimbursement and rewards for good management must underpin the system in order to recognize the significant responsibility and accountability that comes with the new approach.

If all of this is done, then chaos theory can liberate us providing we recognize the new partnership between locality commissioning and health authorities rather than let the 'status quo' be the way forward and thus create the turbulence of organizational dysfunction.

A patient's view

Terry Jones

The immediate problem one faces in providing the patient's view is that there is no such thing as 'the patient'. Whilst GPs, NHS managers and NHS professionals may differ considerably in their views, including their views on locality commissioning, by the very nature of their professional background they have many things in common. In any locality patients have only one thing in common – they are self-centred. This is perfectly understandable since their concern, and that of those involved with them, is about what is happening to them and how their particular problems are, hopefully, to be resolved. But some, of course, have a wider perspective and while still concerned about what locality commissioning can provide for them in times of need, are able to take a broader and, perhaps, more philosophical view.

At one end of this spectrum of patients are those whose knowledge of the NHS is limited to say the least. The only contact most of them have had with the service, if indeed they have had any contact at all, is with their GP and, possibly, those professionals – district nurses, health visitors, physiotherapists – grouped around that GP. They are aware of their local hospitals but many of them will not have to set foot in one unless it is to visit those less fortunate than themselves. Therefore, to them distinctions between 'purchasers' and 'providers' are meaningless – the dialogue at any public meeting about the NHS makes that very clear. It can come as a salutary shock to those working within an organization to realize how easy it is to take things for granted. Certainly many patients in this group become aware of the existence of a health authority only when that authority makes the headlines in the media; normally when there is the proposed closure of a hospital or a reduction in services. If they have a view of the authority at all they see it as remote, isolated in an ivory tower and uninvolved, other than in a negative sense, in what goes on in their locality.

Hopefully, the establishing of locality commissioning groups (LCGs) will overcome some, if not all, of the situations outlined above. If the ordinary patient can be persuaded that these groups will provide them with the best possible services to meet their health needs when those needs arise, then the sense of a 'them and us' situation may disappear. Even those in a locality who have never had to visit a GP will know of the existence of that GP. It can be made clear to them that their GP is going to be personally and closely involved in decisions about the health service provision in their area, decisions which may have a major impact on what can be done to meet their medical needs, where that service will be provided and how this new system will affect them. They are then likely to welcome it even if they don't fully understand it. The term 'advocate', used by NHS professionals about GPs, needs to be clearly defined if patients are to understand that their GP, whilst still 'personal advocate', now has the opportunity to become involved in health services in general in their area. Many will still be self-centred and concerned only about the surgery visit and some will have a cynical view about any change; all will need to be educated about this change.

Indeed 'education' is the key word in any consideration of the views of patients through the whole of the spectrum. There are, in all localities, those who have a much more detailed knowledge of, and interest in, health issues than the 'ordinary patient'. These groups vary widely in composition, interests and background. Some have members who are, in a sense, professionals – the health committees of local councils, locality health and care groups, community health councils and citizens advice bureaux. They are reasonably well informed and can play an important part in putting forward the views of patients in a relatively mutual way, acting as promoters of interests in, and knowledge of, LCGs. They may be able to help LCGs focus on those issues which patients feel need improving and provide feedback on what has been achieved. Other voluntary groups may well have a particular and narrowly focused agenda – one thinks, for example, of Arthritis Care. Members of those groups will need to be persuaded that any change is a change for the better. They may well have very positive ideas and be prepared, when satisfied that their particular concerns have been noted, to take a broad view of the needs of a locality. At least they will have a reasonably well informed view of what LCGs are and what they are trying to do.

Given this range of interests, concerns, knowledge, prejudices what, at the end of the day, do I as a patient expect of this new development and what do I see it offering me that I didn't have before? My view will of necessity be subjective – I doubt any patient will be able to offer one which is totally objective. I will value the parochial (in the best sense of the word) framework of the LCG which will involve people I know, or know of, such as GPs and other local health care professionals. I will appreciate the accessibility not only of those people but also of those who work for the health authority, who can be known in a way in which a chief executive, chairman or Board can never be. I will feel that local interests and needs count whilst accepting that there will always be wider needs, district and national, which will have to be taken into account. But all this depends on the LCG making clear to me, whether as an individual or a member of a group, what it is doing and why it is doing it so that I feel that, within reason, the group is being open. I must feel that my views count, are seen to count and that I have an opportunity to put them forward. Then I can accept that whilst the establishing of LCGs will not bring about a 'new Jerusalem', at least not immediately, it will give me and the other patients out there a better health service.

Reference

1 Singer R (ed.) (1997) *GP Commissioning: an inevitable evolution.* Radcliffe Medical Press, Oxford.
2 DoH/Welsh Office (1995) *Policy Framework for Commissioning Cancer Services.* DoH/Welsh Office Joint Report. HMSO, London.

2 Ten principles for effective GP commissioning

This chapter outlines the ten guiding principles which appear to underpin successful GP commissioning. Some of them have been learned by hard experience. They are not comprehensive but the themes repeat themselves so frequently in the commissioning process that it seems appropriate to list them here.

Principle 1: Ensure that your commissioning group is truly GP led

The early GP commissioning groups were set up by the GPs themselves. They were GP led but sometimes had difficulty in getting the health authorities to support them or listen to them. Health authorities are now becoming increasingly proactive in setting up locality groups and this has led to a rapid increase in their number. For the time being, however, GPs will need to be sure that they are still running the show as they begin to include other members of the primary care team within their groups. There is a danger that they may be 'killed by the kindness' of health authorities who are eager to develop a locality perspective but may develop a top-down hierarchical structure which does not reflect the views of individual GPs in the locality. In locality commissioning GPs should be the leaders just as health authority managers are within their own system. In commissioning decisions the two need to develop an equal partnership, which is adult/adult and not adult/child as it may have been in the past. Health authorities may be reluctant to loosen their control but if they are asking for commitment and accountability from their local GPs then they will quickly realize that this is both necessary and desirable.

GPs are used to being decisive and making rapid pragmatic decisions. Locality commissioning groups (LCGs) may need to proceed at their own pace and not at the rather slower pace that health authorities have previously been used to. Having a leading role means having the greater say in the structure and delegated functions of the commissioning group and being directly consulted on any relevant health authority decisions. This new relationship between GPs and health authorities is bound to have its problems though some friction between the two seems to be productive and can stimulate new ideas and approaches. Locality groups are not simply outreach posts for the health authority and it is important for both patients and member GPs to see that it is they who are dictating the pace.

Principle 2: The commissioning group must be democratic

Only if the group is democratic can it truly and completely represent all the GPs in the locality – this gives it its authority. Furthermore members will only feel bound by any group decisions if they are democratic. If the leading members of the commissioning group are going in the opposite direction to the group in general, then the group must have the right and the power to deselect them and elect true representatives. One of the most common personality types in general practice is 'the lone rebel' and one of the great strengths of GP commissioning is that it has brought GPs together, but they will only stay together if they all feel individually empowered in the process. Democracy, in the words of John Stuart Mill, breeds mediocrity but in reality only those with an interest and aptitude for commissioning have tended to want to lead the process, but it is essential that the grass roots members have a vote in order to stop them going astray. Medical democracy ensures medical accountability and by the same token the commissioning group can engender public accountability by consulting directly with locally elected representatives of the population.

Principle 3: All GPs within the commissioning group should be maximally involved

This does not mean that all GPs should expend time and effort in commissioning but simply that they should all feel that they 'own' the process. This requires great sensitivity on the part of group leaders, who must decide upon those issues on which every member needs to be consulted and on the appropriate means of so doing. The group leaders must remain in close touch with their group and be easily accessible when necessary – particularly so on the few occasions when controversy is likely as one or two unhappy members within a group can be very disruptive. Indeed every group is bound to have what is known as its 'laggards'. Involvement by a maximum number of GPs can be brought about by devolving tasks to appropriate GPs, e.g. looking at clinical issues, audit, needs assessment or liaison with other groups. It is also essential to give them proper time and resourcing to do this. Using the talents of as many members as possible in this way is not only an efficient way of running a group but is also a cohesive process in itself. Talents will also be apparent in the wider primary care team. Involving and using the skills and abilities of practice or fund managers, nurses, other health professionals and attached staff not only makes practical sense but helps to broaden the agenda without diluting the essential involvement of GPs.

Principle 4: Use GP time cost effectively

This means using a minimum of GP time overall and leaving GPs free to do their clinical work. In practice this usually involves the commissioning group delegating work to several executive GPs, or a smaller number of commissioning GPs, with the necessary reserved time to do their commissioning tasks. It also involves GPs in the group in only strategic purchasing and planning, while leaving operational purchasing and planning and day-to-day management issues to the managers themselves. The GPs can also be effectively supported by other primary care team members who are essential reservoirs of information to effect change.

Principle 5: Groups must respect the need for member GPs to be advocates for their patients in the consulting room as well as accountable members of the group outside it

The advocacy role of the GP in the surgery, the practice or even the sub-locality may seem to conflict with his joint commissioning role along with other GPs in the locality. The early working days of a LCG involve building up corporate trust and recognizing the individual interests of member GPs and it is wise, therefore, to look at issues where there are likely to be unitary solutions that benefit all. As co-operative working relationships develop the group may be more able to undertake tasks in areas where the individual interests of GPs may conflict with the collective interest of the group. The commissioning of primary care itself may be just such an issue. The strength of the locality group is that its member GPs should be best able to recognize the conflict of interest between the GP as advocate for an individual patient and the GP as advocate in getting the best services for the local population. The latter collective role is a new one for GPs and will be under threat if the locality group does not deal sympathetically with the traditional and necessarily individualistic attitudes of member GPs. This will be particularly important in the future as the level of demand for, and the level of supply of, services diverge and some commissioning groups begin to take on an increasing role in the prioritization of scarce resources.

If we ask GPs to put their commissioning role in front of their individual patient role then we are in danger of throwing out the baby with the bath water. The strength of GPs in the commissioning process is that they know the patients in the locality well as a result of their consultations with them. At a time when general practice is changing rapidly, nothing should threaten the credibility of a relationship built on mutual trust, respect and intimacy. For GPs empathy, time and the development of a therapeutic relationship with their patients will always be primary to their secondary role as locality commissioners. Some groups are beginning to recognize this as an important issue and in groups where cohesion is strong some are having to appoint ombudsmen GPs to advise on situations where individual GP rights appear to be threatened.

Principle 6: Form an effective relationship with the local DHA

A locality group cannot commission in isolation. It needs to be able to access good public health information and to ensure that its commissioning decisions are translated into effective action via the purchasing plans of the district health authority. Each group will, therefore, have to develop a mechanism which creates a direct link with the health authority (*see* Chapter 4). This may involve the local group appointing a GP Commissioner or Locality Medical Director or possibly appointing members to sit on the health authority or a commissioning sub-committee of the health authority. Whatever the structure, it will provide a means of negotiated decision making which is bound to offer a more constructive approach than the entrenched bi-partisan system that previously existed. In time it is likely that LCGs with their devolved locality management teams will become relatively independent planners with the option of an increased joint role in strategic purchasing. Nevertheless all groups will always need a good working relationship with the centre.

Principle 7: The group should liaise closely with local trusts, specialties and individual consultants

Locality groups should liaise and work closely with local trusts and especially local consultants to become effective. The strength of GP commissioning is in altering the behaviour of local trusts and the attitudes and accountability of clinical directorates. Close collaboration with trust managers and consultants allows mutual exchange of ideas, information and frustrations. The involvement of consultants when discussing specialties ensures that workable and achievable decisions are made and that the clinicians are mutually bound and committed towards any proposed changes. Communicating desired changes to consultants via managers is as inefficient as it is discourteous. Face to face meetings with the consultants need not merely be an expression of what the commissioning group wishes, but can also generate changes in the working practice of both GPs and consultants to achieve mutually agreed aims.

Clearly there are many ways of carrying out this process, e.g. inviting consultants and trust managers to commissioning group executive meetings or having a delegated member of the GP commissioning group liaise directly with individual directorates (*see* Chapters 4 and 7). The actual structure for doing this is less important than the principle that all sides should be fully informed and party to all decisions. By these means it is possible to develop a foundation of trust and a co-operative working atmosphere even though a GP commissioning group, through its health authority, may have the ultimate sanction of deciding where it is going to purchase.

Principle 8: Groups need access to accurate information

Locality groups must have access to accurate information and information technology. Information from health authorities has been notoriously variable and, historically, GP commissioning practices have often lacked the means to access good information. The strength of fundholding has been its good IT access and commissioning too needs accurate information if it is to assess needs, plan appropriately and affect purchasing decisions. Member practices will need advice and financial support in order to purchase appropriate information technology. The locality group will need to take responsibility for integrating these systems and ensuring that they can access appropriate information from member practices, the health authority and the trusts. Deciding how this should be done must be a priority in any new locality group (*see* Chapter 8). Access to information technology, however, is only part of the story. GPs need to develop genuine skills in using systems to inform their treatment decisions and monitor outcomes. Locality commissioning will be underpinned by GPs themselves changing their behaviour to respond to knowledge of what works in primary care. The opportunity for collective work of this sort is one of the most unexplored and potentially most exciting aspects of locality commissioning.

Principle 9: Concentrate on problem areas

This is the principle of 'if it isn't broken, don't fix it'. The greatest benefit is to be derived from having a crack at generally agreed problem areas in the first place. These are the so called 'low hanging fruit'. In this way a commissioning group can have maximum early impact and be most visibly beneficial to member GPs, patients and the local population. No group can fully take over health authority responsibility for planning as it would be quite unnecessary to become involved in all strategic purchasing decisions. Given the limited resources it is only common sense to go for areas where improvements are most needed.

Principle 10: Focus on issues that are appropriately led at locality level

The whole aim of GP commissioning is to make purchasing and planning decisions more locally relevant. Nevertheless, there are whole areas of patient care, particularly those where only small numbers of patients are involved, which are better and more appropriately directed from a larger unit than an LCG because the potential for risk management is better. Locality groups are less likely to do well those tasks that are not locality specific and if they try to take them on it will leave them with less time or resources to look at specific issues affecting the locality. It is good practice for GP commissioning to take on issues which are better tackled collectively at locality level. It is bad dogma to move all planning and purchasing into the locality. In principle, however, if it can be done in a locality then it should be.

3 Getting started

Part One – a GP view

A locality commissioning group (LCG) needs to start on the right footing. It is at this stage that the seeds of trust and co-operation between GPs within the locality must be sown and the key GPs either select themselves or are elected by the group. This is the time when the GPs decide whether locality commissioning has potential or is just another talking shop and/or feel committed, involved, apathetic or even alienated. This is the time when group 'ownership' of the LCG by GPs must be fostered and developed.

The aim of this chapter is not only to help new or fledgling groups but also groups who are finding the going difficult. The assumption in this chapter is that the potential group wishes to go it alone, though some groups have been set up directly by local health authorities and local medical committees (*see* Chapter 6).

Organizing the first meeting

The birth of an LCG occurs at its first meeting – the most important it will ever have. It is also the most difficult as both the group and the agenda will be largely unstructured. Some decisions need to be made before that meeting.

Who is going to call the meeting?

Historically, commissioning groups have been set up by one or two committed local GPs. Frequently the local medical committee has been a catalyst or even prime mover in the process and district health authorities are themselves becoming increasingly proactive in setting up locality groups. This is all to the good but if the aim of this first meeting is to attract as many GPs as possible then it must be remembered that it is their meeting and not the health authority's. It is important, therefore, that one or a number of GPs takes final responsibility for organizing and engendering interest in the meeting.

Who should be invited to the meeting?

The likely size and shape of the locality may be obvious to all concerned but the health authority may have its own pre-conceptions. This may be something that the potential lead GPs and the health authority should discuss before calling a meeting. Considerations include the geography, demography and social culture of the district and there may be an obvious grouping of general practices according to historical associations. It is helpful if the proposed locality consists of GPs who all intend to use the same provider trusts. There is also the question of optimum size which some pundits have put at between 50 000 and 150 000 patients, though many LCGs have performed well with a patient population several times this size.

Time, date and place of first meeting

The proposed meeting must be organized at a time and date when the maximum number of GPs is likely to attend and local knowledge is, therefore, important. The location should be ideally in the centre of the locality and there are arguments for holding it on either GP or neutral premises rather than health authority premises to emphasize that locality commissioning is, in strategic terms at least, a GP-led process.

Who to invite

All GPs in the proposed locality should be invited individually – letters to senior partners are frequently lost – and given a covering letter explaining why it is important that they attend. Practices who do not confirm by a certain date that they are going to attend can be contacted personally. Some would suggest that the practice manager attends this first meeting though there is a danger that the less interested practices may send their practice manager as representative and thus GPs become only peripherally involved. A senior, respected and trusted health authority manager can also be invited and possibly considered a candidate for the role of locality manager if the health authority already has plans in this direction.

The first meeting of an LCG

The first task is to nominate or elect a provisional chairman whose role is to outline the agenda and finishing time and appoint someone to record the meeting. A GP, possibly backed up by a manager (rather than vice versa), can then explain what locality commissioning is about and allow the group to question and debate the issue. If there is consensus about setting up a group then the group will need to define the locality boundaries and elect provisional key GPs to a working party or executive, elect the secretary to the group and seek a contact manager within the health authority. Finally, the chairman needs to fix a date for the next meeting which will have a defined agenda and specify any intervening work that needs to be done.

The first meeting is likely to involve a lot of discussion including as large a number of those present as possible. The aim is to develop a bonding between the GPs and an attitude of mutual trust, respect and desire to co-operate within the group. An additional aim, which can be helped by inviting the right health authority representative, is to sow the seeds of mutual trust between the group and the health authority and emphasize the importance of the group and its potential for effective action.

The next few meetings

The next few meetings will continue the work of the first meeting in terms of developing a corporate attitude among GPs and a better understanding of what locality commissioning entails. It is also important at these meetings to identify and address specific issues as quickly as possible and score some early successes. Groups should ideally:

- look at issues which are of interest and relevance to the majority of the group
- concentrate on what is known as 'win/win' issues, where services are particularly bad and solutions are fairly straightforward. This may involve introducing a new service or improving a present service, e.g. open access echocardiography or a fast track angina clinic. The health authority will need to give strong backing to these early projects in the interests of the future development of the group. At an early stage the group could begin to look at services where money might be saved for use elsewhere as decided by the group, e.g. extra-contractual referrals
- make the agenda interesting – there needs to be a good mix of topical issues and a balance of information, debate and concrete decisions. Nothing kills off an LCG meeting quicker than one speaker, particularly an outsider, talking at length about his or her hobby horse when those present are expecting to debate issues and make important decisions. It creates a balance if the issues raised vary as to their stage in the commissioning process. For instance, some areas should be raised as possible commissioning issues and some planning and strategic purchasing

decisions made. Outcomes are always interesting to the group if they reflect commissioning group successes

- aim for the wide involvement of GPs – they can be involved in tasks such as raising issues, producing consultative documents, sitting on working parties and presenting items at meetings. It is all part of building up a corporate identity in which every individual member feels that he has a role.

The success of these first meetings can be gauged by the atmosphere and level of attendance. The group leaders will also need to keep in touch personally with individual practices to ensure that all is well.

Early tasks

Produce a mission statement

Possibly a little voguish, the production of a mission statement and aims provides a frame of reference and a reminder of where the commissioning process is leading. It can also provide a useful focus for debate at the first or second meeting, *see* Box 3.1.

Box 3.1: An example of a mission statement and basic aims (Dewsbury GP Forum)

Mission statement

To influence the commissioning and provision of primary and secondary health care by communicating the local needs of the community as represented by their GPs.

Aims

- To act as an accessible forum for all North Kirklees GPs and appropriately reflect their views
- To influence and empower the FHSA/WYHA in negotiations with the local providers of health
- To influence and support locally based providers in an attempt to improve the quality, relevance, range, depth and equity of services provided
- To influence long-term planning
- To ensure that the on-going shift from secondary to primary care is properly planned and resourced
- To ensure local needs are met equitably

Create a representational body

Besides choosing a chairman, the group will need to decide on a system for following up group decisions and drawing up agendas for meetings. In one or two groups this is done by one doctor, often the chairman who acts as a commissioner and also as a go-between linking the group, the health authority and other bodies. Most groups have opted to have an executive with each GP on the executive often representing a sub-locality and, therefore, having his or her own constituency. Whatever the system, one GP or group of GPs will be needed to do this work early on in the development of a group and their brief and method of election will need to be specified (*see* Chapter 4).

Relationship to the health authority

Early on a group will need to decide with the health authority how a two-way flow of communication and action plans can be organized in order to make the group effective. There are a number of structures for dealing with this issue (*see* Chapter 4) which vary from one or more doctors sitting on a sub-committee of the health authority to the health authority itself employing a member of the LCG as a part-time manager or medical director.

Formalizing a contract with the health authority

The relationship between the group and the health authority and the expectations of each will need formalizing at an early point as the health authority is ultimately accountable to the Treasury – such a document is necessary if it is to provide funds for locality commissioning. The document does not need to be particularly long or specific but creates a formal basis for commissioning work. An example of such a preliminary document is given in Appendix 2 and considerations for a formal document are given in Appendix 3.

Forming a constitution

At an early stage a group will need to formalize its constitution so that the remit of GPs within the group, their voting rights and the roles of key GPs are all defined. An example of such a constitution is given in Appendix 4.

Getting GPs within the locality involved

The paramount tasks of an embryonic commissioning group is to get its local GPs interested, involved and committed. This is the only way of ensuring that they will become accountable to group decisions, which is a *sine qua non* of locality commissioning. Group co-operation of this sort is relatively foreign to GPs, who have tended to treat their practices as their castles and it is worth repeating that one of the most common personality types in general practice is the 'lone rebel'. GPs are far more likely to demonstrate this streak of individualism and rebelliousness when confronted with what they may see as a health authority driven agenda partly because of the traditionally paternalistic nature of the district health authority. Conversely, they are more likely to develop a group identity in a forum which mainly consists of other GPs and which appears less threatening. This is why it is so important that health authorities allow locality commissioning GPs to develop their own system at their own pace because this provides the greatest likelihood of general commitment to the final outcome.

A study from Middlesex University in early 1997 showed that around two-thirds of fundholders and non-fundholders were happy with the idea of locality commissioning but that a third were not. One reason for fundholders may have been the belief that locality commissioning did not have the 'purchasing bite' of fundholding. It is important for them therefore that an emerging LCG can prove that it does. For non-fundholders the most common objection was that they did not want to have any commissioning involvement whatsoever. Many of these GPs may be living in the hope that the NHS will return to its pre-1990 position before the purchaser/provider split. They will need some persuasion that this is unlikely to happen and that LCGs represent the least of all evils and are better placed than anyone else to make the commissioning decisions that have to be made.

Getting GPs involved in the early stages of an LCG means getting as many as possible to attend those first meetings. Experience has shown that a number of factors are important in getting this commitment and in ensuring high attendance at the meetings, some of which have already been mentioned:

- organize a time, place and date that is suitable for the largest number of GPs. Fix it well in advance at the previous meeting but despatch the agenda a week or two before the next and contact non-responders personally before the meeting
- produce an interesting, relevant and varied agenda. A GP needs to think there will be important information that he needs to attend for and feel

that he will be able to contribute to the debate and that his vote is important. It is helpful to send relevant papers in an interesting and brief format prior to the meeting

- ensure that the agenda and the meeting are GP oriented and led and do not run to a unilateral health authority agenda. The agenda and minutes should be in doctor speak not management speak
- ensure there is a good convivial and collegiate atmosphere at the meetings, helped by pre-meeting food and drinks, which most GPs seem keen to attend for
- ensure some system of payment for attendance – the principle rather than the amount may be important in this respect
- demonstrate in early meetings that the commissioning group has the power to change things for the better and that each individual GP is necessary in this process
- try to involve as many GPs as possible in the commissioning process
- several GPs are likely to be apathetic and a few antagonistic. Talk personally to those who are antagonistic and find out why. Frequently, they will become the most active members if they can see that they have a role to play in the process
- as the group proceeds at least one person should be delegated to ensure that group and executive meetings are keeping in touch with individual GPs and detect and address any negative feelings about the way the group is going.

Relating to the health authority and its managers

Many GPs think, albeit unconsciously, that all managers are supernumerary, in much the same way as many managers must feel that the NHS would run very well without the interruption of doctors. The reality is that the locality commissioning process needs a good working relationship between GPs in the group and the health authority and that it is important to break down boundaries and improve effective communication as quickly as possible.

It is helpful if a senior officer – possibly the chief executive of the health authority – attends the first or second meeting of an LCG to give his or her support and to provide recognition of the group's importance. There should be no hidden agendas between the health authority and the group as there is likely to be an increasing transfer of frequently confidential information between the two. As the working relationship becomes closer and more productive other health authority personnel will need to attend meetings, e.g. the locality manager (if one is chosen), the acute services contracts manager, a manager from finance and others as time and occasion dictate. Getting to know the key players on either side for both the GP commissioning group and the health authority leads to mutual understanding and eventual co-ownership of problems, which is more likely to lead to constructive solutions. This is perhaps the ideal though, in practice, both sides may need initially to challenge each other. For instance, the GPs may need to challenge the health authority if their decisions are not being taken seriously, or if the health authority is not creating the right environment for them to be implemented.

Friction may also occur when the GPs feel that they are being given insufficient autonomy to change contracts or to vire money within the system, either because the health authority purchasing system is too sluggish and non-responsive or because the health authority, with its central perspective, cannot adapt to locality requirements. In these circumstances the GPs may need to catalyse changes within the health authority to make the LCG effective. Conversely, the health authority may need to challenge the GPs showing that if they want a major role in planning and purchasing strategy then they must carry all GPs in the locality with them, so that they are accountable to any decisions made. Such friction between the GPs in the LCG and the central health authority is almost inevitable but managed carefully it can lead to recognition by GPs of a need for greater accountability and recognition by the health authority that it must become more effectively responsive to the demands of its GPs.

The relationship between the LCG and the health authority is a rather hazy one, varying from a large degree of accountability within the health authority and possibly among lead GPs within the LCG, down to a rather undefined and voluntary form of accountability among the less committed within the locality. The haziness of this relationship and the fact that an LCG does not run entirely hand-in-glove with the local health authority, may both be strengths in a system that is looking for consensus within a locality and trying to stimulate a new perspective in the way that services are commissioned. In time, managers begin to respect the intimate knowledge that GPs have about their locality, patients, needs and demands while GPs themselves begin to recognize that managers are an essential part of the commissioning cycle if they want to get things done. Managers tend to be surprised at the consensus that locality commissioning brings while the GPs themselves are frequently surprised at the adaptability and ingenuity of managers to make things happen when they understand properly the GPs' perspective. Like other areas in medicine a good relationship based upon transparency and trust can achieve a great deal.

Engaging with local trusts and consultants

Early in its development an LCG will need to meet with all local acute and community trusts so that they can understand each other's role and the particular issues that the LCG is most concerned with. It helps if the first meeting with a local trust also includes a particular issue that needs addressing, so the trust can be given a positive illustration of the way in which the LCG works and the power invested in it. Trusts will frequently delegate a senior manager whose remit will be to meet with LCGs and who will be responsible for co-ordinating appropriate debate and change within the trust. Prior to such an appointment it may be appropriate for the new LCG to meet with either the chief executive or director of operations and mutually analyse how the trust and the LCG can maintain a future close working relationship.

Where the specialties are concerned, however, it is imperative that consultants themselves are invited to these meetings. Consultants are in the best position to assess the feasibility of any changes proposed within specialties and as the lead players in any change the message often comes better from the GP to consultant than via managers in the contracting process. Frequently, these interchanges between consultants and GPs lead to radical changes in attitude on both sides and bilateral recognition of how services need to be improved and how both can play a role in this (*see* Chapter 7). For instance, a desire to reduce outpatient waiting times may start with the consultants and the trust offering more outpatient slots. It may then progress to consultant and GP-initiated schemes to reduce cancellation of clinics and patient non-attendances respectively. It may end with the development of guidelines and concerted bilateral efforts by consultants and GPs to make the referral process more cost effective and lead to a clearer definition of patients that need referring and those that can be looked after by the GPs themselves.

An LCG can thus facilitate a more mature relationship between GPs, consultants and trusts, where the GPs as commissioners are trying to make the most effective use of scarce resources and where the trusts and consultants are motivated to co-operate with them in performing this task. The forum for these meetings with the consultants can be whole LCG meetings, executive meetings, working party meetings or meetings with a delegated GP or officer of the LCG. Whatever the forum, the presence of trust and health authority managers tends to cement decisions made between GPs and consultants at these meetings.

Keep pace with the group

In the early days there is a danger that the lead GPs will proceed at a faster pace than the rest of the group. If this happens they may quickly lose their mandate and the rest of the group will lose interest and commitment. If this state of affairs continues then the leader of the group will be unable to deliver corporate decisions for which the group accepts accountability and the group will rapidly become ineffective. There are various ways of preventing this:

- ensure that the whole group is as fully informed as possible as to how things are developing. This can be done in meetings of the whole group and also through circulating newsletters and minutes of relevant meetings, e.g. of the executive, working parties or any other developments that are important
- monitor closely the views and attitudes of those most peripherally involved in the LCG to see if they feel they are being sidelined or ignored. Maintain as much personal contact as is feasible
- ensure that any new developments are fully debated and, if necessary, voted upon in meetings of the whole group
- be patient – locality commissioning inevitably involves significant changes in attitude among GPs, consultants and managers. They are right to be suspicious of yet another change in the structure of the NHS but are likely to become more involved and positive if locality commissioning can prove that it is improving the care of their patients.

Part two – a health authority view

A locality focus at board level

The formal merger of DHA with the FHSA took place in April 1996 and was designed to recognize the importance of primary care and secondary care services being planned and commissioned together. There were other changes introduced at the same time; boundaries adjusted, new boards appointed and a revised statutory framework. The overwhelming theme was to ensure primary care was recognized as a key player in the future and that the dominance of secondary care services was adjusted to accommodate a much wider view of health care.

For many on the boards of a health authority working with GP practices, indeed looking beyond the doors of acute and community services, was unknown territory. Locality commissioning has been an uneasy experience for some because it challenged territory that was considered to be a health authority preserve. To explain this further it is useful to look at the different structures of the organizations.

Health authority structure

Health authorities are traditionally structured in hierarchical departments, the boards must have a Director of Finance, a Public Health Consultant and a Chief Executive. The Chief Executive is the accountable officer for the balancing of the books and can be summonsed to the public accounts committee if there are financial shortfalls. Although no longer large organizations, health authorities do have strict management cost targets which are designed to ensure that only a limited proportion of the total health authority budget is spent on management costs. Such targets pay little regard to the needs of a particular authority nor to pay scales, recruitment difficulties and other local factors. A health authority has a contract with the regional office of the NHS Executive and it is required to meet its terms. The performance of a health authority is closely monitored both financially and in the provision of its services.

General practice structure

The nature of general practice is structured quite differently. There is equality between the GP partners who have a financial commitment to the practice and each practice also has a range of directly employed and attached staff. General practice is obviously a much smaller organization and the room for hierarchies and departments less obvious. One of the most striking features of general practice is the sensitivity between partners on the question of individual clinical performance. In health authorities, staff are used to having their performance monitored and discussed but no such personal accountability exists in general practice unless exceptional circumstances should prevail. General practice operates as a small business and to some extent there is competition between practices for patients and an awareness of income generation and cost controls. Health authorities work with financial constraint but are rarely aware of the need to cut costs on an individual basis or in direct ways. All income to a health authority comes from the government; it is never earned and, therefore, income generation is uncommon.

This history of the relationship between GPs, and the old FHSA now health authority is one of contractor status. GPs are under contract to meet the terms and conditions of the the GP Contract and the Red Book. The new world of locality commissioning is grafted on to these old relationships. Many GPs regard with suspicion the health authority which can ultimately hire and fire them and such suspicion can prove a barrier to the early development of positive relationships between authorities and general practice. To overcome these barriers there needs to be clear understanding at both board level and within general practice as to what locality commissioning can offer both parties – adding value to the services commissioned by involving the GP view and local decisions taken closer to where the services are delivered. It can also respond to the needs of the local area and shape it to meet the appropriate circumstances, ensuring that the service is effective in meeting the patient's need and is efficiently delivered in the community. It is important that commitment to these aims is demonstrated by both sides and early discussions on what this means in practice will underpin the first days of establishing locality commissioning. As health authorities set about developing locality commissioning they need to be aware of the possibility of tensions. Successful relationships will be built on the basis of mutual partnerships and not where one party or the other claims superiority of status.

Establishing a locality commissioning model

The development of models for locality commissioning has been led largely by committed groups of GPs and only more recently by health authorities wishing to develop local groups. There is a tendency for health authorities to look for tidy solutions on maps when considering how best to involve groups of doctors. Experience shows, however, that other factors are likely to be more important. GP practice boundaries are not in themselves neat and tidy as they cross district council, county council and urban boundaries. There are two factors that are useful in helping to develop a group – one will be a common trust provider and the second a previously established GP group of perhaps non-fundholders, fundholders or GP co-ops. Strong relationships may also exist around a local hospital or within a town area, but it is perhaps worth noting that some practices may have been formed by breaking away from each other in less than harmonious circumstances.

Where strong groups exist this can sometimes also lead to the exclusion of smaller practices or those on the periphery of obvious centres and negotiation to involve these may be needed. There will possibly be a difference in the perceived cultures of the practices where rural issues are seen to be ignored by urban areas and urban practices who may be concerned with inner city problems have less understanding of the relevance of transport or the allocation of community nurse hours. Finding the right blend of commissioning group is an art and not a science and guidance from the practices themselves will be important. Uneasy groups will be less productive than those where common issues exist. There may be considerable differences between groups within a district area and while some may wish to take on particular responsibilities for budgets or service developments, others may wish to tackle only secondary care issues or act as a sounding board for the health authority.

A difficulty that has yet to be grasped is how much diversity a health authority can tolerate if particular locality groups want to develop services in one direction and this is not supported by other locality groups. The role of the health authority will be to ensure that an appropriate minimum level of service is available to the entire patient population. If an LCG is to truly reflect the needs of the local area then it would be logical to encourage services to develop to meet those needs even if they were not the same across a whole district area.

The health authority role must be to maintain a strategic focus on how services are established but with a local interpretation shaped and supported by local groups. In establishing LCGs a recognition of both differences and similarities requires debate.

Communications with LCGs

For locality commissioning to contribute meaningfully to the decisions of a health authority there needs to be a mechanism for communication between the two. The vehicle for doing this is likely to be a shared strategy (*see* Chapter 6 for a description of how a locality-based health strategy can be developed) requiring an understanding of how policy decisions are drawn up, implemented and monitored. There is also a need for every day communication between the groups and the authority. Some of this can be done via officers and managers but to give the commissioning voice more influence there should be closer involvement in the operational management of a health authority's business. Various models have been developed.

GP medical directors

These include lead GPs usually appointed by their constituency locality group who are offered paid sessional time to work with the health authority on a regular basis. In North & East Devon Health Authority, four locality medical directors work one day a week under an employment contract to the health authority and they are paid at a public health consultant rate. In other areas lead GPs from locality groups are paid ad-hoc sessional fees to attend routine meetings.

Strategy groups

These consist of lead or link GPs with practices whom they represent and form a 'strategy group' that discusses health authority policy and local issues. Again, sessional fees are paid and these groups act as advisors to, and are in effect a sub-committee of the health authority. Groups such as those in Warwickshire have shown the success of these models and GP forums of a number of GP practices or locality groups abound. It is important, however, for the various groups within a district to meet together to share their work and direction and communications will also require some ground rules. If the GP groups are to be representative of their constituent members how do they take on this responsibility on their behalf? Greater involvement in the health authority business means accepting sometimes difficult decisions and being prepared to explain and support these to GP colleagues. The invitation to give advice and take on devolved management of budgets does not mean an abrogation of responsibility when the going gets tough. Lead GPs want to retain faith with their colleagues but they will have to explain their wider commitment. The essential element will be to convince both parties that information is being given and shared honestly. The view that a health authority may have a hidden agenda or additional resources up their sleeve will not make for sensible joint decision making. Similarly, health authorities want to be convinced that confidentiality can be respected when necessary and that a partnership approach to commissioning is exactly that.

Working with LCGs – health authority management arrangements

The very different structures of general practice and health authorities need to be addressed in order to find suitable day-to-day working relationships. The identification of a lead health authority manager or small team is likely to be a good first step in arriving at a way forward. Simply telephoning a health authority without knowing who to speak to about what will never help to further the cause of good communications. Health authorities often appear to general practice as monolithic organizations and GPs are frequently surprised at their comparatively small size and how few in number the staff are. The health authority may be located some distance from the GP practice giving rise to a view of isolation and detachment from its organization. Clearly, practice visiting by managers is part of keeping in touch and a greater flexibility on the part of health authority staff to organize their day makes it easier to fit round the usual pattern of primary care – surgeries, visits, clinics, etc. Face to face discussions and meetings, while an everyday part of a manager's role, will also be dominated by quantities of paper. More used to absorbing policy documents than the average GP, managers need to understand the limitations of excess paper communication. GPs generally work in short frequent intensive consultations that are quickly completed and find the slower discursive policy forming debates, all dutifully recorded in documents, somewhat less than palatable. Executive summaries, clear guidance on what decisions are needed, conclusions to discussions and, where possible, iterative debate will generally be more favoured than a half-inch report.

The joint working of health authority managers and the LCGs will be best realized by understanding how to harness the skills and resources in a health authority – public health, information, financial and contracting activity, locality health profiles, access to research databases – with the more practical responses by a commissioning group on what it is actually like to work with these services in day-to-day practice. Using each other to best effect in this way will achieve the changes the health authorities are seeking and the improvements in services that the practices desire. For these reasons it is useful to be clear at the outset of any piece of work what the expected outcomes of that task are. Problems that can be identified by general practice and are indicative of a wider need to address a service issue will need debate.

It will also take some time for the knowledge of what is possible to be understood. Health authorities are bound by any number of constraints in their management tasks with rules on money and statutory duties. There is no excuse for being unimaginative but there are limitations that need to be understood. Health authorities should not use constraints without explanation but nor should GPs respond naïvely.

Health authorities also suffer from strong political influences. There are media hungry journalists who are also only interested in health stories that are rarely good news and many more columns will be written about possible hospital closures than the development of new services. Because of this health authorities are restrained in the amount of information released. There are influences from the NHS Executive that determine which health authority plans become public knowledge. The health authority's performance is monitored by the NHS Executive and must comply with the corporate contract, guiding those areas of work which have priority and must be delivered. This agenda may not entirely match the issues identified as important by LCGs.

4 Creating a structure

There are probably as many different structures as there are locality commissioning groups and this is exactly as it should be because at present no one model has been shown to be better than another. Furthermore, it is probable that different models are required to cater for different localities which are bound to differ in terms of their patients, GPs and local health authority. The size of the locality, as we shall see, is also a deciding factor in the structure of an LCG. Locality commissioning is about diversity – the differences between the needs and demands of different local populations and the ways that different GP practices operate. For the time being at least, the NHS needs to respect, accommodate and use this diversity rather than impose a top-down uniformity.

It would therefore be inappropriate to propose one generic, 'off the peg' structure to which all LCGs should aspire. As a point of reference, it is possible nevertheless to describe the sort of structures that might develop within the area covered by one DHA as a means of helping GPs and health authority managers decide what sort of model they might wish to have for themselves.

Deciding on a structure

An LCG needs to function on three levels and decisions on structure will need to reflect both group and health authority views on which structure will best cover all three functions.

1 To reflect adequately the views of all or at least most of the GPs in the locality, to achieve consensus in decision making and thereby ensure that individual GPs feel accountable to group decisions.
2 To develop a system which ensures that the wishes of the locality and its purchasing and planning decisions are translated into effective action.

3 To ensure that the LCG co-ordinates successfully with other LCGs in the district and also with the DHA itself.

The structure of an LCG will need to take on other issues such as accountability to the local population and the involvement of other professionals (*see* Chapter 8) but these functions can be accommodated within the structures that follow. Possible structures will be analysed according to these three main functions.

A structure that reflects the views of all or most of the GPs in a locality

This is a prerequisite for GP 'ownership' of an LCG and subsequent accountability. Many LCGs have developed three levels of structure to fulfil this function.

All GPs in a locality

In medium-sized and small localities it may be feasible to invite all GPs in the locality to attend group meetings. This will maximize the number of GPs that can attend (25% attendance would be good, 50% would be exceptional) but it will not work well if only certain GPs from certain practices or parts of the locality attend. The alternative is to invite each practice to send a representative and hope that practices will feel that they are missing out if they do not. Some groups, depending on size, also invite practice managers either as voting or non-voting attenders.

For locality groups that meet as a whole in this way, the group may represent the sovereign decision making body. Important decisions can then be made at group meetings, though a meeting might decide to poll every GP or practice on exceptional issues. Many other groups defer their sovereignty to an elected executive and group meetings then tend to function as a sounding board for two-way flow of advice and information. Meetings of a whole locality group tend to be relatively infrequent, around once a quarter, to ensure that they attend to only the most important and relevant issues and thereby attract maximum attendance. Such attendance by GPs is normally reimbursed by the DHA.

The Executive of an LCG

In many groups the Executive is elected by individual ballot of all GPs within the locality. In large groups, where meetings of the whole group are

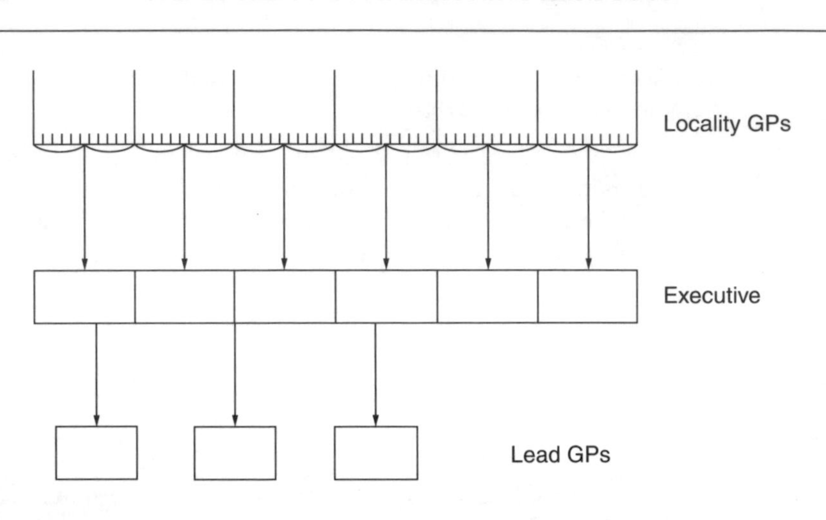

Figure 4.1: A locality group which elects its Executive members on a constituency basis.

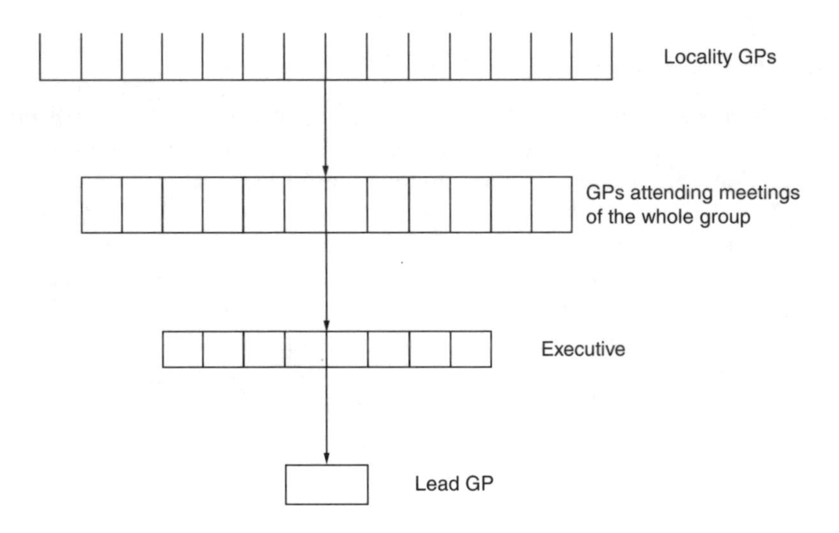

Figure 4.2: A locality group where the Executive is elected 'en bloc' by a group meeting.

impractical, members of the Executive are frequently elected on a constituency basis (*see* Figure 4.1) and thus each member of the Executive is directly accountable to, and voted on by, the GPs within his or her sub-locality. It is then the responsibility of the individual Executive member to make sure that he adequately consults with and represents the views of these GPs. In medium-sized and smaller groups the Executive may be voted in on a constituency basis, by postal ballot of all GPs or possibly voted in at meetings of the whole group (*see* Figure 4.2). In some of the smaller LCGs, the Executive simply consists of an elected partner from each practice. For many groups the Executive is the prime decision making body but for those where this function remains with the whole group, the role of the Executive will be simply to carry forward and implement group decisions.

The number of GPs on an Executive will vary normally between five and 15. Some prefer the tight decision making of a small number while others feel that a larger number is required to be properly democratic. Practice managers are now sitting on some Executives as either voting or non-voting members, sometimes voted in by the mechanisms already described, sometimes nominated following a vote within their local organization of practice managers. Other professionals can be co-opted in this way. All the work of an Executive should be paid for by the DHA and contracts are normally made between the LCG and DHA to enable this to happen (*see* Chapter 3).

Initially, the Executive may be the sole negotiating body of an LCG but this can become impractical as the number of meetings increases and the remit and function of the group widen. Therefore many groups are increasingly relying on a few lead GPs to act as their spokesmen, negotiators and completers and to carry the work of the LCG forward into the health authority itself.

Lead GP(s)

Smaller groups will tend to have a lead GP, often a chairman, who can act as spokesman for the whole group. Larger groups often have several lead GPs taking on various roles such as chief negotiator, secretary and press officer. Increasingly, the lead GP or GPs of an LCG are paid on a sessional basis by the local DHA. This gives them protected time for their work within the group and also for work on behalf of the group and the health authority itself. These lead GPs are thus beginning to adopt a dual role of leading and representing the locality group and also being DHA employees, therefore accountable to the DHA. In some groups these lead GPs are elected by the Executive of the LCG. In others, in order to maintain a strong democratic thread they are directly elected by ballot of the whole locality group.

Early in its development, an LCG will need to specify its preferred structure within a constitution (*see* Chapter 3). The next task of a locality group will be to ensure that from this democratic base it can actually change things.

Developing a structure which ensures that planning and purchasing decisions are effective

Many health authorities have adapted their structures to facilitate the implementation of decisions made by locality groups. They have variously formed core groups, purchasing teams and commissioning boards which are attended by lead GPs from the LCGs and occasionally by the whole Executive of such a group. Increasingly, some LCGs are moving from an advisory role in planning and purchasing to the acceptance of some degree of collective responsibility for such decisions together with other locality groups and managers from the health authority. In some districts lead GPs from the LCGs have seats on the main board of the health authority itself.

Many locality groups have been effective in implementing their decisions using a structure like the one in Figure 4.3. The group has direct access to planning and purchasing decisions within the health authority via its lead GPs, who may sit on a sub-committee or board of the health authority concerned with commissioning. They may also meet directly with managers from the trusts and consultants and can thus directly influence

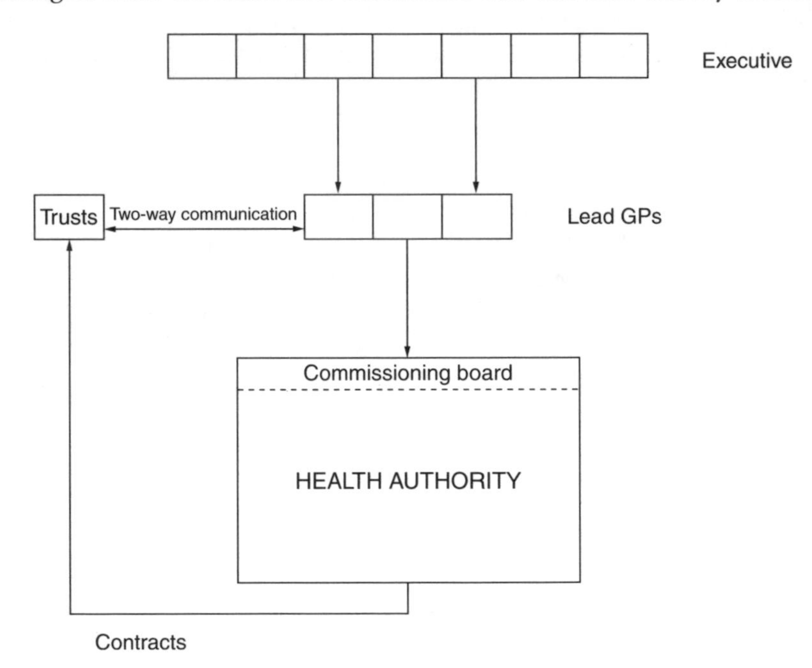

Figure 4.3: An LCG where members of the Executive meet directly with the health authority to influence contracting decisions indirectly.

trust behaviour, or may do so indirectly by clarifying the sorts of messages that they hope to put to the health authority as purchaser. The health authority and trust may also get feedback from managers attending locality group meetings or via their minutes.

As DHAs develop confidence in locality commissioning some are moving to a further stage in the new primary care-led NHS, whereby managers and contracting systems are devolved to each locality, as in Figure 4.4. In this structure the locality has its own locality manager and support staff, its own contracts manager (who may also cover other groups depending on their size) and possibly its own consultant in public health. This enables the group to assess local needs, make joint local planning decisions with its management team, audit the results of its work and give the group a firm basis for the development of primary care within the locality. The same structure potentially allows an LCG a strong role both in making strategic purchasing decisions and in seeing them implemented. A group with this structure can meet local trusts and consultants directly and by having local health authority managers in attendance can use the purchasing process to back these meetings. Where budgets for some or all local services are devolved to the locality management team this allows them to move money flexibly from one service to another and also to alter the pattern of service according to the requirements of the LCG. The health authority in this sort of team structure will still hold the locality budget though there is flexibility for the LCG to take on budgetary responsibility if it so chooses.

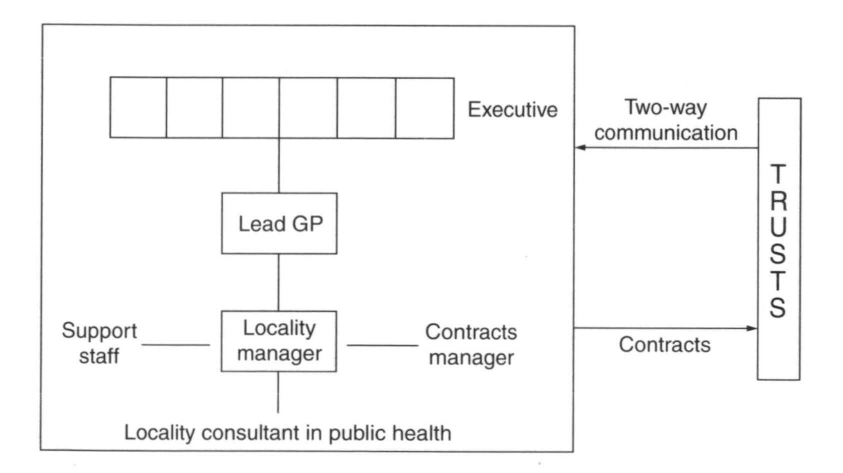

Figure 4.4: A devolved health authority management structure which allows the commissioning group to deal directly with trusts on planning and purchasing issues.

A structure which allows LCGs to co-ordinate with each other and with their DHA

This is a time consuming role, which is being increasingly taken on and developed by lead GPs from LCGs. They have a range of titles from 'lead GPs' or 'GP commissioners' to 'locality medical directors' and their job specification is enlarging as locality commissioning develops. Their prime role is to liaise with other GPs and managers involved in locality commissioning and Figures 4.3 and 4.4 both allow for a locality commissioning board where lead GPs in the localities and involved managers can meet (Figures 4.5 and 4.6). The role of the board is not only to co-ordinate activity but also to exchange information and ideas as well as to share work. For instance, one LCG which takes on the task of planning and purchasing future district nursing services can offer the results of its work for use, possibly in a slightly adapted form, to another LCG which is then free to work on a different project. As well as interacting with each other there needs to be a structure for the lead GPs to interact at all other levels within the health authority and with all of its directorates in implementing the primary care-led process. Much of DHA work involves the dissemination of centrally driven, bottom-down directives and the lead GPs are becoming increasingly involved in passing these down the line to the LCG. Inevitably they end up performing two roles, which may be potentially contradictory

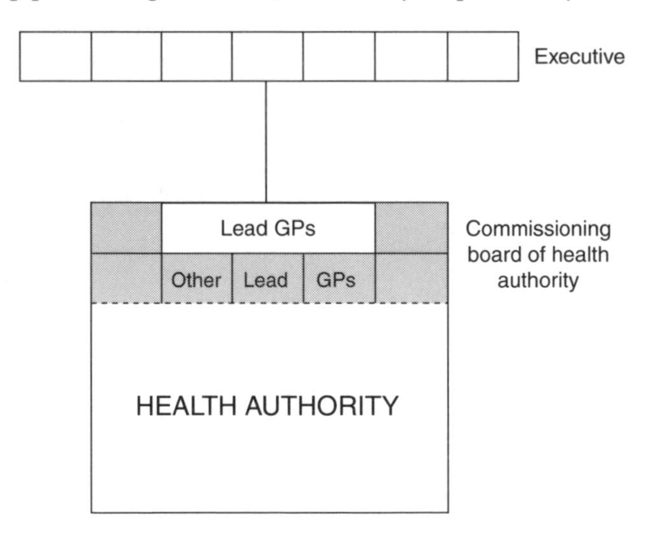

Figure 4.5: A structure which allows lead GPs of LCGs to co-ordinate with each other and with their DHA.

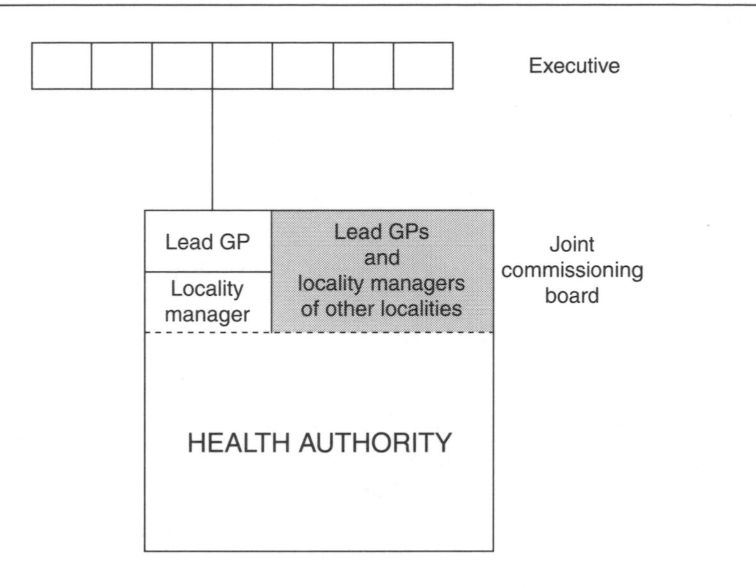

Figure 4.6: A structure which allows devolved management from a health authority and lead GPs in the locality to interact with other localities and the health authority itself.

– that of representing the bottom-up and democratic decisions of the LCG and that of being facilitator for centrally driven bottom-down messages from the DHA. They may become vulnerable when arbitrating between the two different kinds of agenda but this vulnerability and their dual role is also one of the greatest strengths of such a locality structure.

Summary

A few general themes emerge from this analysis of possible structures for LCGs. These are illustrated in Figure 4.7. Most have a representational system that is described within circle A and which is aimed to ensure that the lead GPs and Executive of the group truly represent the views of individual GPs in the locality. Commissioning decisions are also covered by circle A in the early days of an LCG when it has a largely advisory role. As it begins to engage more with the DHA and in cases where the authority is happy to delegate managerial staff to deal with LCG business an effective commissioning process requires the LCG and managers to work closely in a structure that involves all key players within rectangle B. The LCG, a locality body, is not directly accountable to the central agendas of the government, NHSE or the DHA, but the key players in square C are. These will include the lead GP or GPs who have contracts with the health

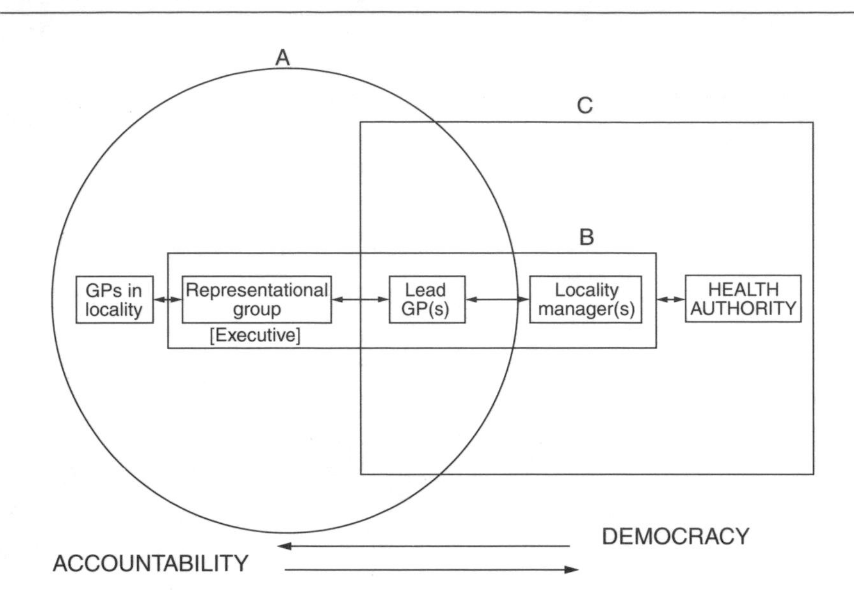

Figure 4.7: Interrelationship between the three functions of an LCG.

authority and who work closely with its locality management team. Figure 4.7 shows how the lead GP or GPs within an LCG are pivotal in ensuring that a group represents the views of its GPs, is effective in its planning and any strategic purchasing activities and fits properly within the context of the DHA and its more centralized priorities.

The interface between the lead GP or GPs and devolved locality managers is crucial for the success of such a combined GP/health authority operation. The lead GP needs to ensure that the locality managers keep faith with the wishes of local GPs, who elected him or her, yet at the same time he or she must deliver a locality Executive that accepts that there are other priorities as well as local ones. The accountability of a GP not particularly involved in the locality is bound to be less than individuals further up the line such as the Executive, the lead GP or locality manager. The in-built elasticity of this system is, however, its strength as the lead GP or GPs and the locality manager can act as shock absorbers when messages coming up from locality GPs and coming down from the health authority conflict. Health authorities may feel uneasy about devolving or even relinquishing control to such a loose network but are beginning to see that they are gaining a degree of accountability among ordinary GPs that they never previously had and the GPs for their part are happy to provide this in return for having a real say in how locality services are organized.

What happens if things go wrong? What if LCGs cannot deliver the goods? This is a pertinent question for health authorities, who may interpret these structures as involving the hand-over of a lot of control without the promise of a great deal in return.

On the democratic front, if the group loses confidence in the Executive or lead GPs they can simply vote them out. Things are more difficult if conflict means that issues cannot be resolved by the LCG and this may require the health authority to take back the right to make decisions at least in certain areas.

In terms of influencing decisions, if the LCG feels that the health authority is only paying lip service and is not concerned about putting structures in place that facilitate the group's role then the LCG may wish to withdraw from the relationship. This did indeed happen in the early days of LCGs when some health authorities were unwilling to recognize them but is a rare occurrence nowadays. In its third function – to co-ordinate with the centre – the group can disengage from its close relationship with the health authority if it feels that the health authority is trying to impose unreasonable and unpopular agendas on the group.

The most common tension that is likely to arise in the future will concern underfunding and the willingness of LCGs to co-operate in the task of prioritizing services. This may require LCGs to accept that some services that they feel to be necessary cannot be offered within given financial constraints. They may simply reason that they are prioritizing services rather than rationing them and that if there are insufficient funds that is the fault of the central authorities. Alternatively they may feel vulnerable, when surrounded by a population of patients and other professionals, who feel less accountable to the distribution of limited funds. In some circumstances, if there are insufficient funds for a group to provide a minimum level of services, the LCG may need to appeal to its DHA. The health authority will then have two options: on the one hand it can agree with the commissioning group and refer the problem on, or on the other, it may feel that the group has got its priorities wrong and will either need to persuade the group that this is so or take back some of the commissioning role and thus disempower it. Either way this makes rationing a transparent process and it offers patients and the NHS an important and possibly a sole safety valve when services are being cut too thin.

The structure chosen by any LCG and its health authority is important but the personalities involved and their motivation are even more important. This is why structures should be chosen to suit local GPs, patients and health authorities and why they should not be imposed.

Examples of locality commissioning structures and their successes

The examples given here are far from comprehensive and omit a number of important groups and structures, which may be equally as good or better. There should be enough, however, to show that a wide range of different structures can produce success.

Large LCGs (150 000+ patients)

The Nottingham non-fundholders commissioning group has been one of the most successful groups and has possibly one of the most complex structures.

Established in 1992 and covering 200 GPs, the group has set up a constituency system for representation on its Executive (*see* Figure 4.1), which is broadly based on social service boundaries. The Executive GPs are paid by the health authority for their involvement and in the absence of meetings of the whole group must ensure that they represent and communicate with individual GPs in their constituency. As in Figure 4.1 a number of GPs on the Executive form an inner Executive of lead GPs who co-ordinate with the health authority and local trusts in a way that has some similarities with Figure 4.3, though the actual model is far more complex and is depicted in Figure 4.8. The lead GPs have input to purchasing decisions via the Nottingham Health Authority purchasing teams. They are separately involved in planning through two systems. They sit on the medical advisory committee, which brings together representatives of all GPs, trust clinicians, a public health doctor and a representative of the medical school in order to look at medium- and long-term planning objectives. They also liaise directly with the four health authority directorates of women and children's health, surgical specialties, general medical issues and mental illness and substance abuse. The group initially concentrated on improving secondary services particularly waiting times and ENT, orthopaedics and ophthalmology with varied success. More recently they have concentrated on primary care with an innovative scheme of integrated practice nursing, district nursing and health visiting and another scheme which provides early intervention with expert physiotherapy for low back pain. They have also introduced practice-based coagulation monitoring for which GPs are paid per patient monitored. The group has also demonstrated a role for commissioning groups in both controlling prescribing costs (which are 7% lower than the national average) and as drug purchasers, including the bulk purchasing of vaccines. The group's

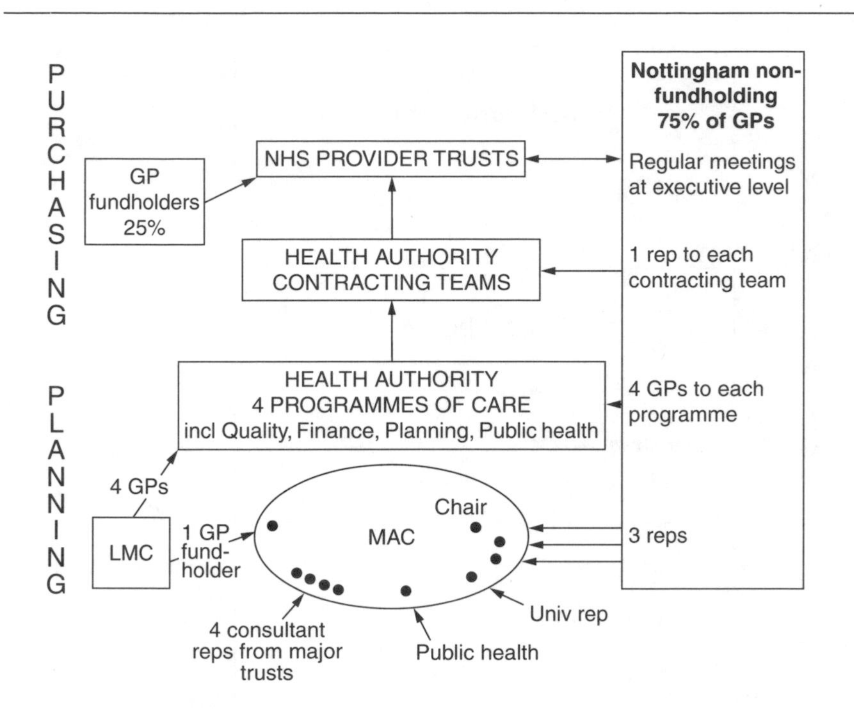

Figure 4.8: The Nottingham model.

metamorphosis into the Nottingham Total Commissioning Project involves a change to the structure shown in Figure 4.9 and which represents a change from the general structure shown in Figure 4.3 to one more like that of Figure 4.4 at the beginning of this chapter. One of the important consequences of this change is that, in the words of the group itself, it will allow 'shared responsibility between the Nottingham Health Authority and a core group who are elected representative GPs for the deployment of Nottingham Health Authority's budget within an agreed accountability framework'. The words here are important, LCGs are not purchasers nor do they wish to or actually hold any budgets for themselves. It remains to be seen whether sharing responsibility for the deployment of a budget in this way will make a commissioning group more effective. Though it should be an option for some, it should never be compulsory for all (*see* Chapter 7).

Another large group, the Blackpool, Wyre and Fylde GP Advisory Group was founded in 1991 and covers a population of 320 000 patients. Like the Nottingham group they have an Executive, which consists of representatives covering nine constituencies of around 20 GPs each, whose main role is to liaise with GPs in the locality in order to find out their needs

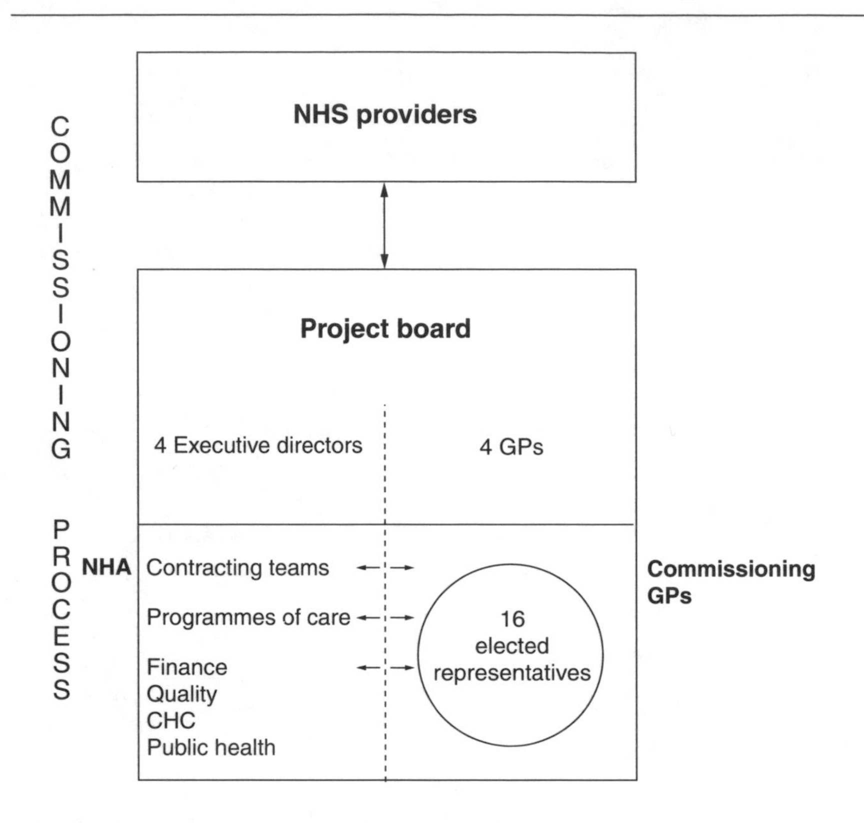

Figure 4.9: The Nottingham Total Commissioning Project.

and problems and convey this information upwards. Each representative also has a liaison role with providers with each one having a responsibility for one or two clinical directorates. Their representational structure is similar to Figure 4.1 and their purchasing mechanism similar to Figure 4.3 though all the Executive, not just lead GPs, meet with the commissioner board of the health authority six times a year. The chairman of the group is also a full member of the health authority commissioner board. The group has been influential in reviewing psychiatric services and developing a number of new services such as a post-myocardial rehabilitation programme, open access echo-cardiography, a surgery-based dietetic service and a pregnancy assessment unit. It has also been instrumental in generating changes where there are no financial implications such as a locally based lithotripsy service.

The Dewsbury LCG (Figure 4.10) is one of three within the catchment area of the West Yorkshire Health Authority and covers a slightly smaller population than the other two groups of around 170 000 patients. This

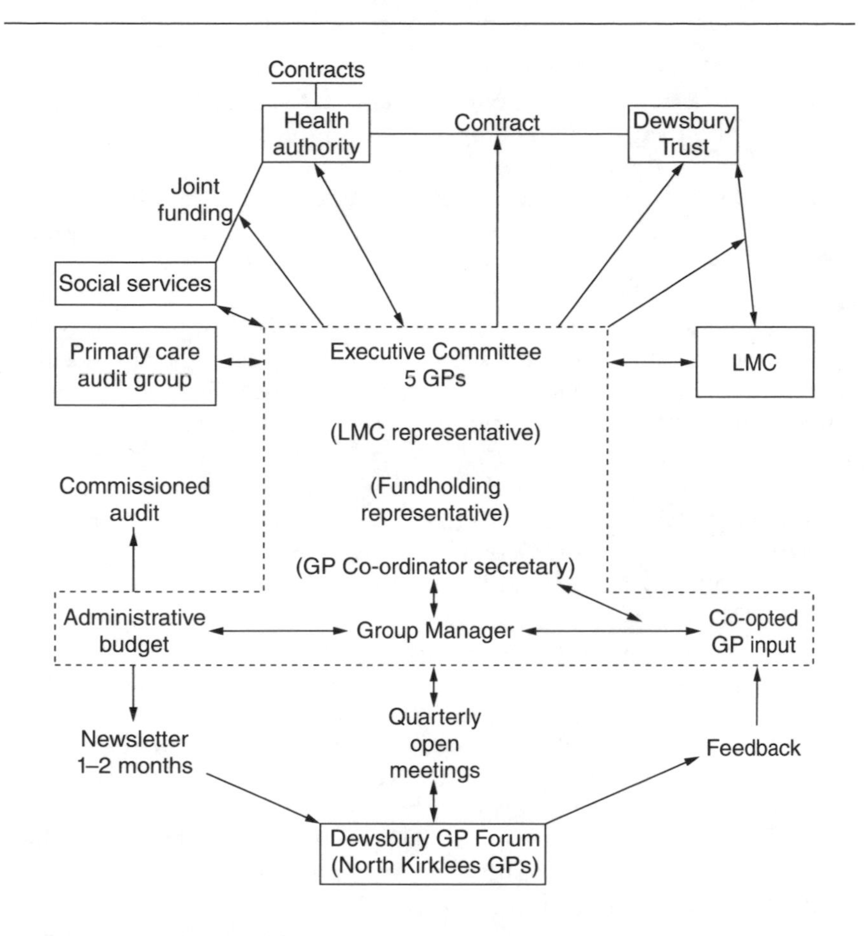

Figure 4.10: Dewsbury model.

allows it to have quarterly meetings of all GPs within the group and it has a strong relationship with the LMC and primary care audit group.

The group also has strong links with other local GP commissioning groups in Huddersfield and Calderdale and has been involved in agreeing quality criteria for contracts, introducing day-case surgery, practice-based service level agreements and leading a project on care for the elderly in the local community.

Medium-sized commissioning groups (50 000–150 000 patients)

The four LCGs within the North & East Devon Health Authority all fall within this range and have structures conforming to Figures 4.2 and 4.4. The Mid-Devon GP commissioning group is one of these and was formed in early 1993 covering 95 000 patients. Each practice is paid for attendance at the quarterly whole group meetings and each of the six Executive members are paid for attending monthly meetings. The lead GP or locality medical director works for two sessions a week paid for by the health authority and both he or she and the Executive are all elected by meetings of the whole group on an annual basis. The locality medical director liaises closely with the locality manager for Mid-Devon (employed by the DHA) and the two act as an important route for the transfer of information and decisions upwards and downwards (Figure 4.7). The locality medical director and locality manager for each locality meet up with their opposites from other localities and liaise directly with other Directorates in the health authority. Devolvement of health authority structures to locality level allows the commissioning group to commission primary and secondary care and also to meet directly with trusts using the same structure. Like the Nottingham group the Mid-Devon group has primarily concentrated on secondary services and reduced waiting times for outpatients, inpatients and investigations. Lack of money within the health authority has limited this purchasing role, which now has to concentrate on cost-neutral improvements within the trust. The group has also introduced a locality scheme for admitting elderly acutely ill patients and reduced unnecessary extra contractual referrals within the locality. It is now more involved in planning issues such as the re-build of a large community hospital, the future provision of terminal care and the way in which work is distributed between primary and secondary care.

The Small Heath LCG covers 120 000 patients and the North Birmingham Community Health Trust has allocated a senior manager specifically to liaise with it. It has an elected board of 14 GPs representing each practice. The group has worked closely with social services to develop a system where GPs make direct appointments for their patients with a named social worker. The group has also set up a black minority ethnic working group, a fast track angina clinic, fast track access to 24-h ECG, echocardiography and exercise ECGs and made an agreement with the local trust for catheterization of male patients.

Small LCGs (around 50 000 patients or less)

In Dorset, a total population of just under 700 000 patients is divided into 14 localities. The structure in East Dorset is similar to that in Figure 4.1 where each practice is invited to send a representative to the locality group meetings. The localities in the east vary in size from 25 000–75 000 patients and each locality is represented by its chairman, who is paid for a session a week. The chairpersons of all of the localities meet together with a GP commissioner (a part-time manager) at least every eight weeks to share information and to advise and influence the health authority on issues that apply across localities. This core group committee also identifies actions which can be taken by single locality groups in order to avoid unnecessary duplication of their work.

The locality chairman and GP commissioner also sit on the East Dorset Commissioning Board which is the main medical advisory board to the health authority. This board meets on a quarterly basis and includes the chief executive and other executive officers of the health authority. It is chaired by the chairman of the commissioning group and it is envisaged that this will be expanded to involve representatives of West Dorset, and this larger strategic board would meet twice a year to advise on issues which cover the whole county, e.g. cardiac surgery and cancer services. This structure has resulted in the production of locality plans for most localities in the eastern part of Dorset and there have been considerable improvements in secondary care services, especially dermatology, neurology and orthopaedic services. An interesting facet of this group is that it is both a large commissioning group (covering 285 GPs and 482 000 patients and eight parliamentary constituencies) and, at the same time, consists of six smaller locality groups. The group is presently negotiating for open access CT scans and has accepted, as a quid pro quo, that GPs should gain prior accreditation in their appropriate use.

In Bromley, the health authority (Figure 4.11) appointed eight clinical commissioning directors to cover eight locality areas varying from populations of 25 000 to around 60 000.

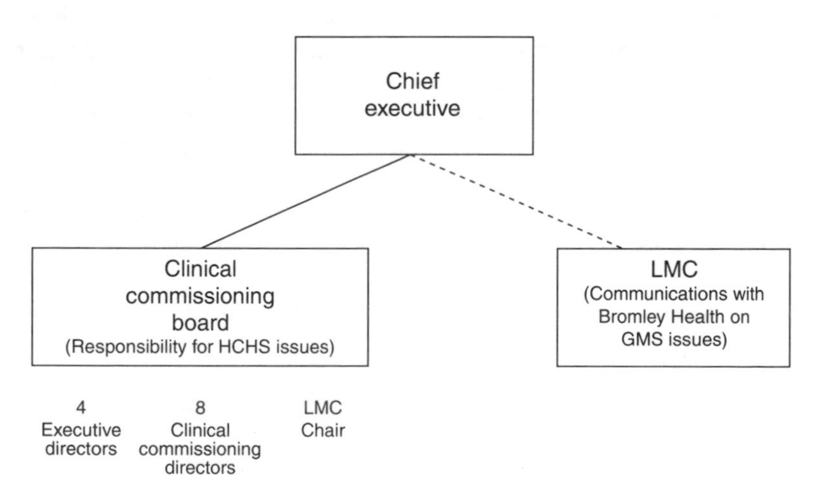

Figure 4.11: Bromley model.

The role of the directors is to help the authority make decisions about local health services and to meet up and to communicate with GPs from within their locality. The GPs are paid for one management session a week and the board meets twice a month.

The structure is similar to that in Figure 4.1 but there is no Executive group in each locality and directors represent localities but are not elected by them. Localities represented by the GP clinical commissioning directors, therefore, do not yet have LCGs but this model is seen by those involved as a 'useful staging post before moving into locality commissioning'. As a health authority driven model it provides an interesting way of introducing the concept of locality commissioning to a district where grass roots GPs may not be initially interested. Though the structure has only been up and running since 1995 it has already been involved in useful work on prioritizing areas for new investment and planning future mental health services.

In Birmingham, in addition to a total purchasing pilot and the Small Heath GP group already mentioned, there are three smaller commissioning group projects – Hall Green GP Commissioning Project (40 000 patients), Kings Norton/Northfield (which has rapidly increased from 22 500 patients to 63 000) and Selley Park (31 000 patients) – as with the Small Heath group these groups do not have meetings of all GPs within the locality but every practice nominates a partner who sits on the Executive or Board. Each board produces its commissioning intentions and the health authority is currently developing a 'weighted capitation' formula to calculate locality commissioning budgets. Once these are in place the contracting process could eventually devolve from the health authority commissioning teams towards GP commissioning groups and the health authority organization is evolving to reflect this process. The groups have improved access times to orthopaedics, catalysed screening for eye disease in diabetic patients by community optometrists and been involved in improving rheumatology, developing integrated nursing teams and prioritizing mental health.

Though many commissioning groups started off small, there are few small groups left. The groups in Birmingham are rapidly expanding and the groups in East Dorset form part of a large commissioning group. The current pilot scheme has not accepted applicants covering fewer than 50 000 patients and this appears to follow the trend in GP commissioning.

Relationships with other GPs and professionals

LMC

The relationship between LCGs and their local medical committee (LMC) is variable. Some groups relate very little apart from exchanging minutes of meetings while other groups are part of their local medical committee. The Enfield and Haringey GP Commissioning Executive (GPCE), founded in 1993 and covering 110 practices and nearly 500 000 people, has seven members drawn from the LMC Executive, who are the only directly elected representatives among the 13 GPCE members. In November 1997, the group had six directly elected GPs according to geographical area, as well as five LMC members. It co-ordinates closely with the LMC, CEGP (continuing education for GPs) and PCAG (primary care audit group). The result is a group that can catalyse and co-ordinate the various processes of audit, education and commissioning as well as the role of GPs as providers of services. The group has taken responsibility for setting up standards in general practice and has been instrumental in setting up one-stop clinics and trying to define in co-operation with consultant colleagues, post-hospital discharge responsibilities. One interesting feature of this group is that it meets with consultants in one specialty from different trusts when considering clinical issues rather than seeing each trust and its relevant consultants separately. This may be an approach that is more appropriate for a larger commissioning group.

Another group in Cambridge and Huntingdon (Figure 4.12) has been set up entirely by the LMC. The GP electorate chooses LMC representatives on a constituency basis and the LMC itself chooses a core of lead GPs with responsibility for negotiating and liaising with the health authority. In some ways this simple model is similar to the pre-1990 situation when LMCs chose GPs to sit on the district management team and main board of a health authority. The difference in this structure is that more GPs are involved in negotiations with the health authority than before and their negotiating position is far stronger. It is likely that in future LCGs will be increasingly initiated by health authorities (as in Bromley) or by LMCs (as in Cambridge and Huntingdon) and less, as in the past, by local groups of GPs deciding to work together.

LMCs have an increasing role in representing the interests of GPs beyond general medical services and the publication of the GMSC's non-core strategy reflects the LMC's role in guiding GPs on the transfer of work from the secondary to primary sector within the commissioning process. Successive LMC conferences over the past few years have vigorously supported the role of LMCs in representing the commissioning interests of GPs. Given that LMCs are the only statutory representative body on behalf of GPs and coupled with the increased remit of general practice beyond traditional GMS, there is a strong argument for commissioning groups to keep in close contact and retain links with their LMCs. LMCs may also have a part to play in negotiating the non-core budget and contractual agreements between LCGs and health authorities.

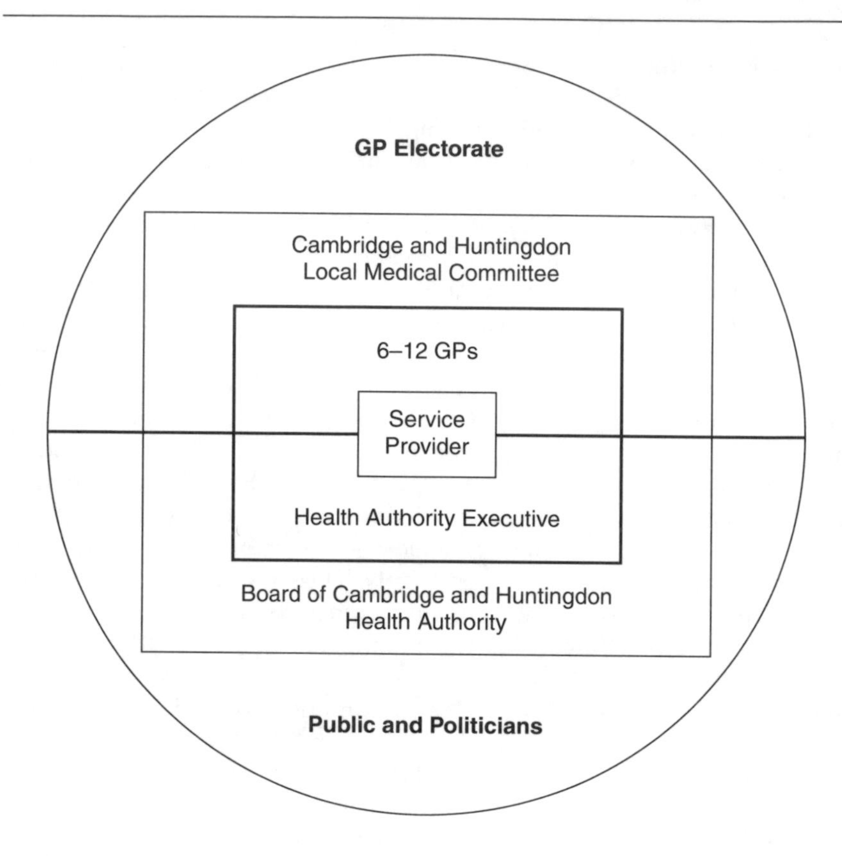

Figure 4.12: Cambridge and Huntingdon model.

Working with allied professions

A few LCGs have practice managers on their Executive but hardly any have included other professionals. The Langbaurgh Coast GP Commissioning Group (LCCG) covering 58 000 patients was set up in 1994. It has a board of directors consisting of 11 GPs, two district nursing sisters, one health visitor, one representative of professionals allied to medicine (PAMS), an executive director of the local community and mental health trust, an executive director of the local acute hospital trust and an executive director of the health authority. Everyone on the board has a vote. LCCG has always been GP-led and is now a primary care-led commissioning group working in partnership with community staff, the health authority and the two main providers. LCCG has been and continues to be successful in commissioning quality services from its two main providers. Eventually, it is assumed by some that GP commissioning and locality commissioning will give way to commissioning by the primary care team. Few structures include this vision at present, which makes this group particularly interesting.

How do the allied professionals themselves regard the concept of working with LCGs? Clare Landymore, a practice manager who sits on a GP commissioning group states:

> 'I was very privileged to be voted by the practice managers working in our locality to serve as one of the two practice/fund managers on the Executive Committee of our locality commissioning group. It was fascinating for a practice manager to be asked to join a forward thinking group of GPs tackling the politics and pathways of the Health Authority and Trust. Nevertheless, several aspects need to be addressed by the managers in the locality:
>
> (i) The two elected managers must meet regularly with other managers in the locality
> (ii) GPs and managers within the individual practices will need to communicate internally with each other. Not everyone can attend all the meetings and continue to function in individual roles in the busy primary care team
> (iii) GPs and managers should consider how to disseminate information at this time of change for the whole primary care team
> (iv) It is important that managers within a locality feel safe enough to start sharing information across practice and professional boundaries
> (v) As locality commissioning progresses, further members of the primary health care team will need to be involved in some way with the functioning of the Executive Committee. There will need to be a process in place to integrate these professionals sensitively into the workings of locality purchasing.
>
> My first meetings as an Executive member of our locality commissioning group have left me with a feeling of being positive about the future of primary care teams and the role of the manager – I definitely want to be part of the locality work.'

Again and again the message is about co-operation and good communication within a wide variation of structures. Structural diversity is necessary within a developing system and most of the groups described in this chapter are now formal pilots (*see* Chapter 10) with central funding. It is above all the desire of GPs, health authorities and trusts to co-operate and improve things, which will define the success or otherwise of an LCG. If there is a good structure for doing so, then so much the better.

5 Who needs needs assessment? Assessing health needs and integrating public health into locality commissioning

Virginia Pearson

Why assess the need for health care?

Equal access to health care on the basis of need is one of the fundamental principles on which the National Health Service was established,[1] and which has permeated health policy to the present day.[2] The concept of equity – equal access to health care services for those with equal health needs – is enshrined in this, although there is evidence that health care needs have not been equitably met,[3] and recent publications have highlighted the persistence of variations in health.[4] What general practitioners and other health care professionals want for their patients are the highest quality health services possible within available resources: this means services that are acceptable and accessible to patients, that are effective, and represent value for money.[5]

What is needs assessment?

Needs assessment is the bringing together of two strands – information about the health care needs of the population, and evidence about what health care interventions do (or do not) work[6] – and combining these to produce a series of objectives for improving the health status of the population, which can be measured in terms of mortality (e.g. a standardized mortality ratio), morbidity (e.g. admissions for coronary artery bypass grafts, termination of pregnancy or fractured neck of femur), or other health status measure (e.g. by using a validated questionnaire such as the Nottingham Health Profile or the SF-36). Changes in health status can be measured with progress through the health care system (Figure 5.1).

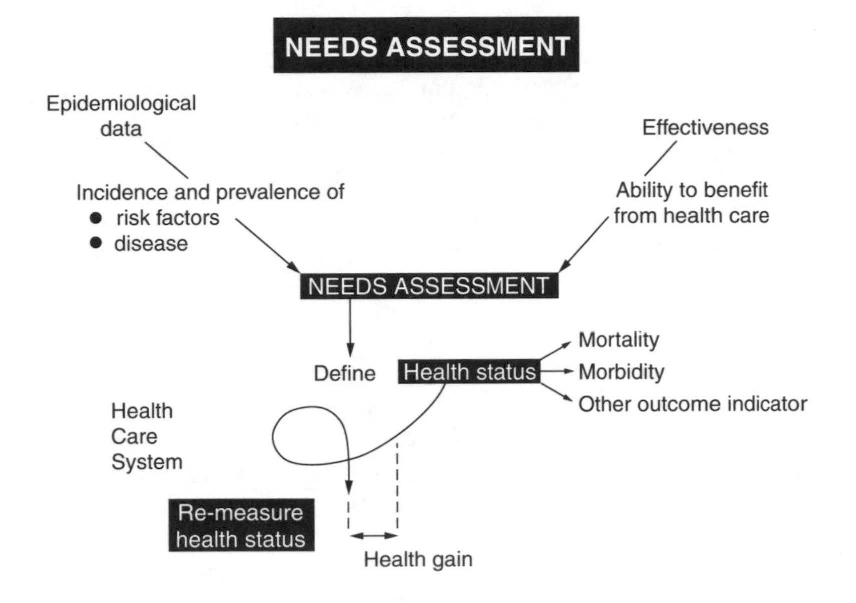

Figure 5.1: Measuring health status.

What does public health have to offer?

Public health physicians specialize in population health. The major review of the public health function undertaken by Acheson in 1986[7] confirmed the importance of assessing the health needs of DHA populations. It ensured that the proper long-term planning of health services, which involved addressing the issue of unmet health care needs, became part of health authority work. Every health authority therefore has a public health department where there will be a pool of knowledge and skills which should be readily accessible. As well as specializing in population health, they will be able to access information on evidence-based health care, provide a wider view of the picture of health services within the district and the locality plus likely future developments, and can help in developing a strategic focus.

GP groups are taking on increasing responsibility for the commissioning of health care services. They will need professional support in local needs assessments and information on how health varies among the main populations of the district. These are part of the broader, long-term view that public health brings to the commissioning of health services. Options for formal public health input include a public health consultant or specialist registrar becoming involved with LCGs and assisting in the commissioning process. Alternatively, they may be involved on a district-wide basis by having responsibility for a particular care group or condition. As a relatively scarce resource, they might also be used for training GPs and primary health care staff in health needs assessment and applied epidemiology and helping them and members of the primary health care team to use their own data. This might be the most cost effective option in the long run and allow public health physicians to provide extra support as and when necessary.

LCGs and public health

Issues surrounding health promotion or the early or long-term prevention of disease may seem a long way from more immediate quality issues, such as waiting times for elective surgical procedures or communication between secondary and primary care. These short-term issues need to be complemented by the medium- and long-term plans for commissioning health care over the next 3–5 years, in conjunction with district-wide policies, so that all the resources for health care within the district are mobilized towards the same goals. As we move closer to devolved budgets for commissioning, just because health service monies are distributed equitably on the basis of resource allocation formulae, it does not mean that they are spent equitably.[8]

A major task for locality commissioners is to disentangle the important issues from the less important ones in health care terms – no easy task. This is where public health's experience of looking at the 'big picture' is essential. Many health care professionals and lay people will feel that health authorities are bureaucracies, giving them little opportunity of influencing how money is spent.[9] In reality, patterns of spending are largely historical and the only way to change this is to review thoroughly the appropriateness of the existing resource allocation for a particular specialty, care group or condition. Although time-consuming the opportunity cost of *not* reviewing areas of major investment and just purchasing 'blind' could be considerable.

Primary care teams have a wealth of knowledge and experience in health care which can be used in assessing need and planning the future shape of health care. Unfortunately, there are several barriers to the full integration of primary care into the commissioning process. It is therefore important to generate a sufficient level of interest in the process and to show primary health care teams that involvement leads to real change and that structures exist for facilitating the involvement of GPs.[10]

Needs assessment is the first step in the commissioning cycle (*see* Figure 1.1, p. 4) and if locality commissioning teams are to influence health care policy setting and planning then they need to not only contribute to, but undertake, needs assessment themselves. The level at which the assessment is undertaken will determine the level of influence: some issues may be relevant for a particular practice (e.g. a large nursing home or a travellers' site in the practice area) but would not necessarily affect the whole locality or district. Nevertheless, changes can be implemented at a practice level which may be straightforward organizational ones, but which can improve the quality of health service delivery.

How do we measure the health care needs of our population?

There are now a number of useful publications which explain different methods for assessing health care needs.[11,12] The most frequently used techniques include: using routinely available public health statistics in combination with local provider activity data; information from national disease-specific or *ad hoc* surveys; participative techniques with community 'key informers', such as rapid appraisal; and the use of practice information.[13] Each of these techniques is useful for different aspects of health need, and may also have added benefits, such as mobilizing a community in support of a health issue. However, all health needs assessment requires time and effort, and local ownership of projects, and involvement of those who can effect change, is essential if the process is to be of value. Advice may need to be sought on which are the most appropriate techniques to use, and which data are already available. Sharing of experiences by practices within a locality or district may also save time and energy.

Although public health departments will have a wealth of data on mortality and admissions to hospital, the data lack the immediacy and detail of information available in primary care.[14] Much primary care activity is taken up with conditions that are important determinants of avoidable death and disability, such as hypertension, diabetes and musculoskeletal disorders such as osteoarthritis and rheumatoid arthritis. The advantage of accessing this primary care activity data is that it gives a valuable indication of future trends and is thus an essential part of planning ahead.[15] Validity of data is a potential problem but an investment in ensuring that the data held on computer in a practice are accurate is repaid with information that is timely, relevant to the practice and can be monitored readily for clinical audit purposes.

Presenting primary care teams with reams of statistics is unlikely to enthuse them: looking at their own data in conjunction with readily available information will be far more relevant. Many public health departments have ready access to small area statistics and can offer the necessary support and expertise in interpreting information (remembering that random variation will occur with small numbers and can produce wide year-on-year variations).

As well as activity data, practices also have access to other sources of information. For instance, employed and attached staff will have access to qualitative as well as quantitative data which can inform an assessment of need for a given population. This can be an option for GPs who do not want to or cannot do it themselves. Project 2000 nurses educated to degree and diploma level may carry out a needs assessment project as part of their studies, so it is becoming increasingly likely that each primary health care team will include someone with the required skills and who could lead a project or help others who are interested.

Although for many this will be new territory, the outcome will provide the locality group with a wider view of the health needs of a population rather than just its individuals. This is always a dilemma for those in hands-on specialties or professions: however, it is our responsibility as part of all those working in the NHS to recognize that we do not work in isolation, and that our activities will always affect others in the health care system. Conversely, health care interventions are taking place that do not necessarily impinge on every individual health care professional (e.g. organ transplantation, specialist rehabilitation or forensic psychiatry): they are still an essential part of the health care needs of the population, even if, at a practice level, they are only encountered once every five years. Learning to view the population as a whole as well as recognizing the needs of people on an individual basis raises issues about how variations or inequalities in health are tackled. While the concept of 'horizontal' equity is familiar (equal treatment of equals), applying a concept of 'vertical' equity requires a much more sophisticated understanding of meeting health care needs. This might involve having to decide on a weighting that should be applied to health service provision and access to ensure that health gain is greater in those with poorer health,[16] directing health promotion campaigns at women at greater risk of cervical cancer,[17] or targeting antenatal care to those women in the lower socio-economic groups.[18]

How do we meet health care needs?

Health care needs assessment must be rooted in the real world. To effect change, the outcome must be a series of objectives that can be met, by the practice or by others, in an agreed time frame. Although many of the changes may be internal (practice) ones, there must be a fair and explicit system for feeding the results of the needs assessment into the commissioning cycle and thus influencing external forces for change: the LCG and the health authority. Practices, locality groups and health authorities need an agreed agenda for prioritizing whatever new resources are available, and for shifting resources from areas of little or no health gain to those where real benefits can be achieved.

The fictional example that follows shows how one practice with problems in the management of coronary heart disease carried out a needs assessment to help them improve the health of their population, but also helped the health authority and the LCG define one important area for action.

Scenario: The Fore Street Practice, Portchester

This practice, with a list size of 12 500 patients, had the highest standardized mortality ratio for coronary heart disease (CHD) in the district, and this was significantly higher than expected for its age–sex structure. The local public health department had produced scattergrams correlating mortality from various diseases against admission rates and, unexpectedly, the practice found that it had one of the lowest admission rates in the district despite having good access to the nearby hospital. Postulating that this represented unmet need, the practice team decided to investigate. The practice nurse led a small in-house group looking at the management of CHD in primary and secondary care. The public health department provided admissions data for CHD by age band, plus information about the expected incidence and prevalence of CHD for the practice population; the practice manager carried out a search of the practice computer system using the relevant READ codes, and other practice staff contributed to assembling an accurate practice register.

There was a significantly higher number of people with CHD than expected in the 45–65 year age groups. The practice population consisted largely of people from the lower socioeconomic groups, and, from the few records containing lifestyle information, there appeared to be a high proportion of smokers. Having determined the prevalence of the condition in the practice, one of the GPs contacted the local public health department for information on effective interventions for CHD. The practice had difficulty finding information about the prevalence of risk factors for CHD in the practice: although diligent in completing records when the old health promotion scheme was initiated, things had lapsed. In addition, the practice nurse contacted the local primary care audit facilitator for help and advice, as two recent primary care audits were helpful: one on prescribing of low-dose aspirin after myocardial infarction showed that only 45% of patients were taking it, and a recent audit of thrombolysis (chest pain-to-needle times) indicated that performance could be improved.

The small working group decided that a number of factors were important in meeting the needs of their population: internal changes were required such as improving the quality of risk factor data held by the practice and abandoning the time consuming 'well man' clinics operating two sessions a week in favour of a structured recall system for the management of hypertension and hypercholesterolaemia in the practice (Figure 5.2).

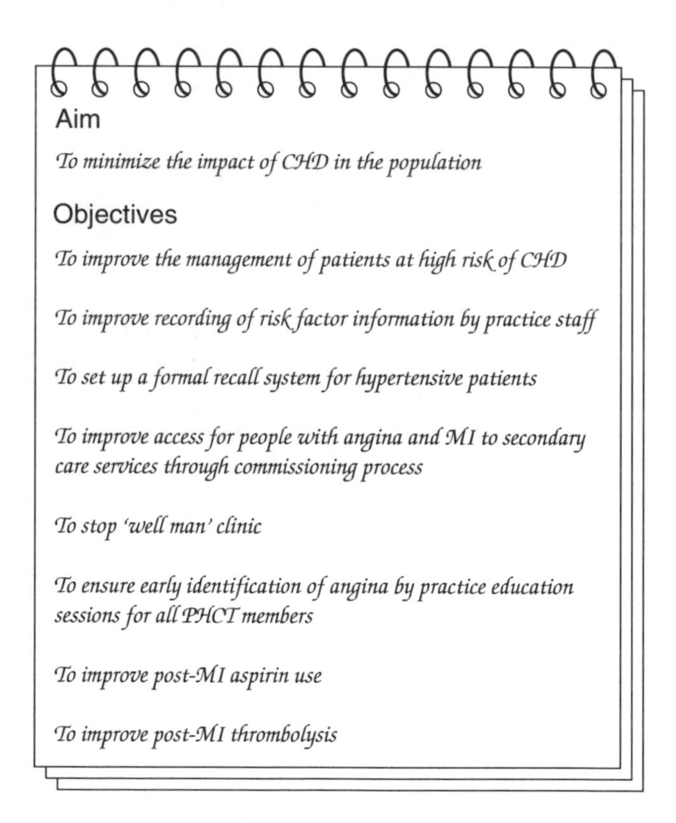

Figure 5.2: Objective setting.

The LCG was asked to commission the local trust to provide an open access chest pain clinic at the local hospital to negotiate 10% more coronary artery bypass grafts in the coming financial year at marginal cost and to develop a locality-wide strategy for promoting the use of nicotine patches for smokers. This last suggestion involved not only practice but also health visitors and community pharmacists in combination with a local campaign to reduce smoking in public places. Having generated some interest in the practice for tackling smoking, the practice midwife and health visitor were concerned about the high numbers of pregnant women smoking and the frequency with which GPs were seeing children with upper respiratory tract and middle ear infections. They agreed to lead the next needs assessment on the health of infants and children in the practice in order to see how all the resources available to the practice could be best utilized to the benefit of this group.

The inequity in provision of services for CHD across the district was raised by the LCG as a main item for review and it became one of five major projects for the health authority in the new commissioning cycle. At a practice level, the team was able to demonstrate real improvements in its management of risk factors for CHD as well as the diagnosis and management of angina and had a significant improvement in the number of people who were admitted to hospital with myocardial infarction over the next 12 months and who received aspirin post-infarction. The needs assessment was adopted as a model for other practices with significantly high standardized mortality ratios.

Summary

Making public health an integral part of locality commissioning ensures that commissioning occurs within the overall perspective of total health care provision for the population. It also ensures that there is a fair and explicit system for debating priorities in health care. Needs assessment, by virtue of its processes, ensures that issues surrounding the acceptability, effectiveness and cost effectiveness of health services are included. It enables the locality commissioning process to make a major contribution to the health authority's overall commissioning cycle, ensuring that major service change is driven by the need for health care.

References

1 Beveridge report (1942) *Social Insurance and Allied Services, Command Paper 6404*. HMSO, London.

2 NHS Executive (1997) *EL(97)33. Changing the internal market.* Department of Health, Leeds.
3 Tudor Hart J (1971) The inverse care law. *Lancet* **i**: 405–12.
4 Variations Sub-group of the Chief Medical Officer's Health of the Nation Working Group (1995) *Variations in Health. What can the Department of Health and the NHS do?* Department of Health, London.
5 Maxwell R (1984) Quality assessment in health. *BMJ* **288**: 1470–2.
6 Stevens A, Gabbay J (1991) Needs assessment needs assessment. *Health Trends* **23**: 20–3.
7 Department of Health (1988) *Public Health in England* (Acheson report). Department of Health, London.
8 Mooney G (1996) Resource allocation and aboriginal health. *Australian and New Zealand Journal of Public Health* **20**: 9.
9 Will AM (1995) Contracting is a recipe for inefficiency. *BMJ* **310**: 60 [letter].
10 Morley V (1993) Empowering GPs as purchasers. *BMJ* **306**: 112–4.
11 Harris A (ed.) (1997) *Needs to Know: A Guide to Needs Assessment for Primary Care.* Churchill Livingstone, London.
12 Buton P, Harrison L (eds) *Identifying Local Health Needs: New Community Based Approaches.* The Policy Press, Bristol.
13 Murray SA, Graham LJC (1995) Practice based health needs assessment: use of four methods in a small neighbourhood. *BMJ* **310**: 1443–9.
14 Pearson N, O'Brian J, Thomas H, Ewings P, Gallier L, Bussey A (1996) Collecting morbidity data in general practice: the Somerset morbidity project. *BMJ* **312**: 1517–20.
15 NHS Executive Information Management Group (1996) *Collection of Health Data from General Practice: Overview.* NHSE, Leeds.
16 Jan S, Wiseman V (1996) Equity in health care: some conceptual and practical issues. *Australian and New Zealand Journal of Public Health* **20**: 9–11.
17 NHS Centre for Reviews and Dissemination (1995) *Review of the Research on the Effectiveness of Health Service Interventions to Reduce Variations in Health.* University of York, York.
18 Clarke LL, Miller MK, Vogel WB, Davis KE, Mahan CS (1993) The effectiveness of Florida's 'Improved Pregnancy Outcome' program. *Journal of Health Care for the Poor and Underserved* **4**: 117–32.

6 Planning

Prior to 1990 and the NHS and Community Care Act, health authority planning was a flowing river over which GPs had little influence. The source of this river where plans originated was a forbidden land, as unknown to the local population as it was to other health professionals and GPs. GPs were represented at the estuary on district management teams and health authority boards but were little able to influence events by this stage. The 1990 Act made things if anything worse as district management teams were disbanded and GPs were swept off health authority boards. Locality commissioning represents a grass roots attempt to redress this imbalance and put GPs, other health professionals and the patients themselves back in the planning role. This is only logical if the NHS is to be truly 'primary care-led' and for the first time GPs are beginning to find themselves at the very source of where plans are made.

Planning is the sequel to assessing the health needs of the local population (*see* Chapter 5). It is a quite different process from specifying exactly what is to be purchased and from whom, which is itself the next step on (*see* Chapter 7). Nevertheless, as we shall see, discussions on what sort of services are to be purchased may often become mutual discussions on short-term planning as the two processes are interconnected in any mature relationship between a purchaser and a provider. Longer term planning will become easier as the internal market is replaced with more collaborative arrangements. Service agreements will replace an annual contracting round and these will give more scope to develop collective agreements on how services will change over time.

We have already seen (*see* Chapter 4) the diverse ways in which LCGs may be involved in planning. In some the whole locality group is the sovereign body. In others an elected executive is the main working unit and in several it is lead GPs who are mainly responsible for this process. The interface with the local health authority may be a sub-committee, special commissioning board or even the board of the health authority itself.

Some lead GPs in commissioning groups negotiate directly with the individual directorates of a health authority and some are involved on combined advisory bodies such as a medical advisory group. Some health authorities are beginning to produce locality specific strategic plans and some are devolving their managers to localities so that they can co-operatively produce locality plans with their LCG. The great challenge of the next few years will be for LCGs to show that they can produce good quality locality health strategies which can be equally owned by other health professionals and the local population.

LCGs will be mainly involved in planning for their own localities. The greater part of this chapter will therefore be devoted to how groups can develop a locality health strategy using any of the structures outlined above. Groups will also need to be involved in decisions at district level which may also affect the locality. Finally, they will also need to co-ordinate their planning with local trusts. This chapter will analyse all three planning roles and look at how they can be integrated to provide a unified health service.

Developing a locality health strategy

Good health and health care are dependent on the actions of many agencies and groups within and without the NHS. A locality health strategy is designed to draw these elements together and encourage agencies to approach their tasks in a coherent way. The health needs of the locality can be identified from a range of data but for most people good health will also reflect their social, environmental and general quality of life. Indeed people often find it difficult to distinguish the boundaries that are erected between one agency and another. A locality health strategy is a way of ensuring that these barriers do not get in the way of providing a co-ordinated, effective and efficient range of services in a community.

Health authorities and NHS contractors have a statutory duty to provide a range of services. This includes making sure that resources are spent on services for people that need them and which provide the greatest possible health gain for the local population. To discharge these duties it is essential that information and plans are shared and developed together. Within the locality health strategy there will be a need to address the national priorities which the government of the day determines as essential to be delivered by the NHS. There will also be a need to address the joint areas of work and priorities developed with social services and the housing department in particular and with other agencies such as the police, probation and education departments. There will then be opportunities to address areas of local priority that respond to the particular needs of their area. This may vary between parts of the locality and through a sensitivity to these issues a strategy to meet them can be drawn up.

The primary aim of a locality health strategy is, therefore to:

- get closer to the needs of local people and focus on areas of greatest need
- increase responsiveness to local circumstances
- strengthen accountability to the people served
- develop partnerships with both statutory and other service providers within the area
- implement national, district and local priorities.

The health authority planning cycle

The health authority has an annual programme that is determined by the NHS Executive in order to meet budgetary and planning deadlines. Health authorities are required to decide how their resources are to be spent in partnership with provider trusts. Approval to proceed with these plans will then be confirmed by an agreement between the health authority and the NHS Executive. Regional offices review health authorities against this for satisfactory performance to ensure that resources are spent as detailed and services are delivered according to plan. For this they will want to have information on the service and financial framework in which services will be provided and developed.

LCGs need to understand something of how this planning cycle works as they will have to observe the same deadlines and where budgets are devolved they will need to work within the same financial constraints and target dates. A locality health strategy will provide the framework for the planning cycle and will illustrate the input of the various agencies at critical consultation periods. However, a strategy should not be just about the short-term actions. It should look further ahead to a planned programme of priority setting making longer term changes to the way services are delivered. A shared view of where the service is going will be the strategic aim of a locality and this will depend on the many factors that contribute to its delivery: resources, acceptability, effectiveness and competing priorities. A locality health strategy is an opportunity to make some attempt to look at the issue of prioritization for services. The NHS is cash limited, it cannot meet all the demands made upon it. This means choices have to be made. Rarely is the choice between a service or no service, it is rather a choice between how much is made available to a particular service. Restricting access to a limited number of patients by waiting lists is a well understood mechanism for containing costs but there are other ways in which services are targeted to particular groups. A locality health strategy will need to express the priority areas for that locality in order to target those considered to have greatest needs. This will require a consultation process which feeds into the planning cycle. Health authorities' cycles always work April to March, a year in advance. Therefore, planning takes place in year one for delivery in year two. However, it is not helpful to think of planning as something only undertaken during certain months of the year. The process for an LCG should be drawing on information all year round, and formulating ways of dealing with change. Some of these may be quickly resolved, others will need to take a longer term view. Figure 6.1 below gives an overview of how the planning process works.

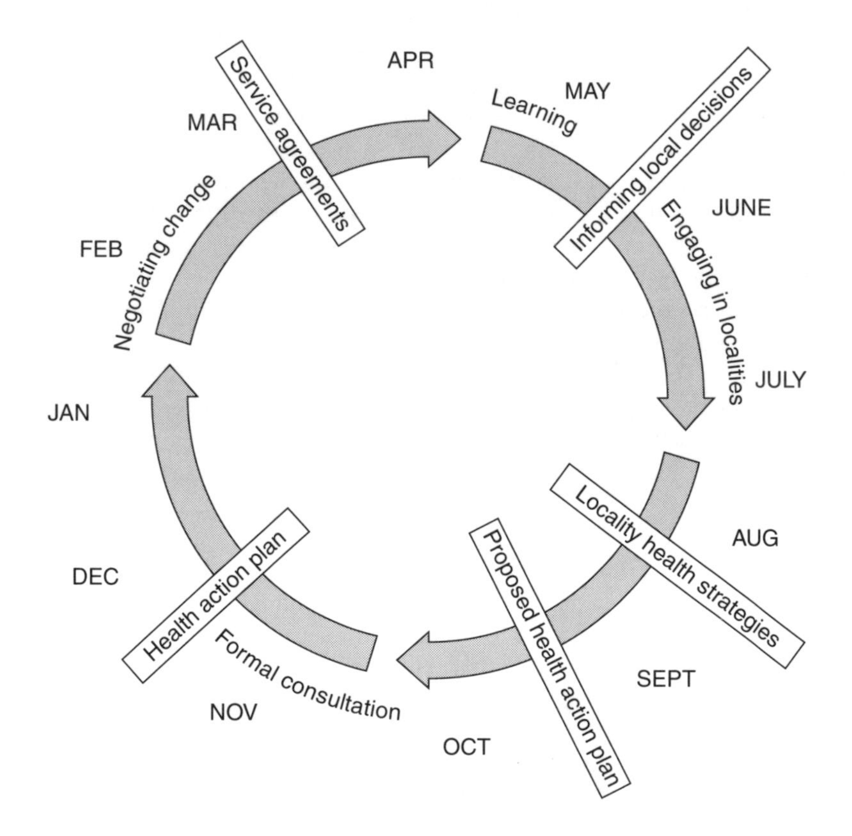

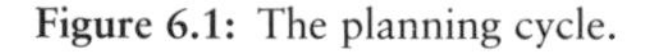
Figure 6.1: The planning cycle.

Planning cycle

The first quarter will see the conclusion of:

- reviews and audits of the previous year's work. This gives a chance to look at what was achieved, what was learnt from the previous year and where changes need to be made
- annual reports made including the Public Health Report, Patient Charter Report, Health of the Nation Report. These latter two will also identify targets for achievement that must be met in the following year
- priorities and strategic review of social services and the housing strategy. These will both be published including the Community Care Plan which will set an agenda of jointly agreed areas of work between the agencies
- information gathering from local groups of what needs to be in a purchasing plan. This is sought from Joint Consultative Committees, CHCs, voluntary groups and the private sector
- practice reports which are returned at the end of this quarter.

In the second quarter the planning for the district takes place and this is drawn into the service agreements. This should identify:

- locality priorities that have developed from the information over the year and from the reports received in the first quarter
- information about the resource position to see what is going to be possible and affordable
- phased programmes for strategic priorities that have been delivered over a period of time
- action areas where local provider trusts have highlighted concerns, service pressures and changes need to be introduced
- information about clinical effectiveness reviews that may address certain technology, drugs or treatment options that will need to be adjusted.

The service agreements will be key documents for health authorities as they will set their programme of work for the following year and place this within a service and financial framework for longer term strategic change.

Some health authorities have produced locality plans. As part of their strategy, they will include the national, district and local priorities and resource allocations. They will also refer to implementation proposals. It is certainly an option for the locality to include in the purchasing plan some locality specific purchasing plans or strategic intentions. A purchasing plan, however, may not reflect the full picture of the locality.

In the third quarter consultation on the plans takes place. This should:

- invite feedback from patient groups, providers, contractors and statutory agencies on the proposals and invite comment on the effects of these policies for their agency
- work in partnership with provider trusts where short and longer term changes are likely to be made
- stimulate new areas for review for completion in time for this or subsequent planning cycles
- establish the action plan for the next year to meet the plans outlined.

In the fourth quarter all the service agreement plans will need to be finalized. There will need to be:

- agreement of the specifications of the services to be purchased including service and quality standards
- a plan for the activity, resources and the profile of service delivery for the year
- the funding associated with service delivery
- the monitoring arrangements
- longer term strategic objectives
- jointly commissioned work with social services and others which is agreed and a review agenda which is decided upon for the next 12 months
- joint finance bids which are approved on the recommendations of the Joint Consultative Committees
- agreed fundholder budgets.

The planning cycle is based on a fairly simple structure of plan, implement and review. There are opportunities for input and influence at many points on the wheel. The trick is to handle the information and develop a coherent strategy that meets the many influences upon it.

Using information

At practice level

In the previous chapter, the availability and use of public health data were discussed. The sources of this data are variable some being extremely accurate and informative, others being less specific and easy to apply. However, the advantage is that such data are presented in a form that is very locally targeted. The demonstration of these data will engage practices in the locality who will be able to see their own practice performance, their needs profile and the individual outcomes from their practice list rather than being given data that are general and district wide. It gives opportunities for practices to see the bench marks for their performance as well as seeing the needs of their practices in a bench marked form. Practices can then assess if they have unusually high instances of, for example, coronary heart disease or diabetes and compare that picture with the locality as a whole, the district and even national distribution. The use of such data within practices is one of the critical elements of successful locality commissioning. It gives practices the opportunity to look carefully at their patients' needs, at their response made within the practice to meet these needs and most particularly to stimulate a discussion on how to address and plan to improve services in primary care. An example of how this might look in practice is given in Figure 6.2.

A locality health strategy will then be informed both by the data on practice performance and also by the steps taken by practices to address their needs. It will be the basis for commissioning decisions to look at where service shortfalls are identified and where changes need to be made in primary, community and secondary care services. The collected views of practices will build up a picture of how services should be shaped. This process gives support to the practices to reflect on their particular circumstances and to see their issues as generally shared by others and gives opportunities for taking coherent action to meet them. We will see in the next chapter how an LCG can be an effective influence on providers. A similar strength can be found to tackle some of the issues for primary care by the identification of shared problems. However, to arrive at such a point does require commitment by practices to look critically at their own performance and to take steps to seek solutions or options and discuss and share these with others. The development of practice plans will be an important one in ensuring that the locality health strategy includes the areas of work that are important to primary care. Too often purchasing plans developed by health authorities are dominated by secondary care issues of little obvious relevance to practices on a day-to-day basis.

At locality level

It becomes quickly obvious in the preparation of a locality health strategy that many of the issues that arise are due to circumstances beyond the immediate scope of primary care. These may be problems of poverty, poor housing, unemployment and the many aspects of deprivation that can affect health. While no health strategy can expect to solve all the problems of society, an attempt to share and match the steps taken by other agencies

LOCAL NEEDS ASSESSMENT

DISEASES WITH HIGHER THAN AVERAGE DEATH RATES IN MID-DEVON

Although the Mid-Devon population is generally healthier than some other parts of the United Kingdom, there are five health problems where there are some statistically significant variations. These are: Stroke, Breast Cancer, Skin Cancer, Accidents and Diabetes. More detailed data is highlighted below:

STROKE

The mortality rate from strokes is statistically significant in Canonsleigh (SMR 178.9), Bridestowe (SMR 167.5), Castle (SMR 151.8) and Cullompton (SMR 131.2). Overall, the actual number of people dying from strokes is fairly low, about 130 per annum in the whole district. Strokes however, are a cause for increased morbidity (disability) and a cause for admission to hospital. High rates of admission are found in the Cullompton area, Okehampton and Tiverton areas.

ACTION POINTS:
- Focus on preventative health education.
- Participate in integrated care management project.

DIABETES

Mortality rates from diabetes are higher than the rest of the district and nearly twice as high as East Devon. Recording diabetes as a cause of death is rather unusual and clarity on how these deaths are recorded on the death certificate needs to be investigated. Admission rates for diabetes are also the highest in the district with a rate of 6.01 per 10 000 compared to a district average of 5.61. Additionally, Mid-Devon has the second highest rate of admissions for diabetic coma. Obesity is a contributory factor and nationally this is a trend that is increasing.

ACTION POINTS:
- Focus on data collection to review screening procedures.
- Participate in project regarding diabetic screening of feet.

ACCIDENTS

Mid-Devon has a higher rate of death from accidents in young people under 15 than our other localities. The rate is almost 4 times that of East Devon and one and a half times the district average. The types of accidents most common in those under 15 include:

- Falls – 161
- Transport accidents – 73
- Poisoning – 64
- Machinery or instruments – 45
- Environmental factors – 35
- Striking objects or persons – 33

In all, 459 children had accidents in the period 1992–1996 requiring admission to hospital and 7 died during 1989–1993. Areas that have particularly high admissions include Taw Vale (213), Sandford (149), Exbourne (132) and Lawrence (112.6).

ACTION POINTS:
- Urgent action is needed to address these concerns. Education programmes on hazards need to be reviewed.
- It is noted that children under 5 years old are particularly at risk. Assistance with safety equipment in the home needs to be established.

BREAST CANCER

126 women have died from breast cancer in the period 1989–1993 in Mid-Devon. For women of all ages this averages 3.85 per 10 000 of the population. However, in the age group 50–69 years, the rate is 8.41. There are very low numbers in many ward areas but Cullompton and Crediton show the highest levels. Mid-Devon has almost half the number of admission rates to hospital compared to North Devon.

ACTION POINTS:
- Focus on ensuring uptake for screening services is sustained.
- Commission an analysis of deaths in target areas.

SKIN CANCER

Mid-Devon has the highest rate of deaths from skin cancer in the district. The SMR rate is 148.9 with a national average of 100. The actual number of people dying was 23 in the last 4 years. There is much that can be done to prevent skin cancer. This rate is higher than much of England and Wales, and indeed higher than some areas of Australia.

ACTION POINTS:
- Focus on continuing education programmes about risks and symptoms.
- Review some case histories to see if further guidelines are needed.

Figure 6.2: Sample page on needs assessment taken from a locality health strategy.

may be a positive way of improving services in a local area. Many of the services have elements of health, social care and housing that will impact upon each other. A simple example will be the discharge of a patient from a community hospital – their co-ordination of assessment, rehabilitation services and safety at home will be vital to provide an effective service to the patient. Understanding why it is important to discharge promptly, why assessments need to be undertaken, and how homes can be prepared for a patient's return will be to respect the agencies' various positions and to work collaboratively to achieve each other's outcomes. A locality health strategy can be a vehicle to explain how these services need to be planned together as a means of promoting interagency co-operation.

At individual level

A locality health strategy built up from the constituent parts of the available data ought to include the views of the people for whom the services are commissioned. The views of individual service users, carers, voluntary groups, representatives of local communities, statutory groups, such as CHCs and JCCs, will all provide a voice of what the priorities are for the locality. It will be especially important when using a locality health strategy as the basis for commissioning decisions to consider the effectiveness of the services as perceived by the patient and also to identify the quality standards that are important to them. Patient views can be sought in a number of ways and efforts to establish networks within a locality to have access to a collective or individual view will contribute to the development of the strategy (*see* Chapter 9). The locality health strategy is designed to knit together the elements of many parts and propose actions to meet the different agendas. No one element will provide the whole picture by itself.

At national level

Making use of information from a national set of priorities will be a 'must' of a locality health strategy. This will list the politically driven agenda of the government and the trick for the strategy will be to plan the implementation of these priorities in ways that are sensitive to local needs. It may be that a priority around AIDS or drug misuse will be important for an inner city area but less important in rural Devon where the continuing care needs of elderly people (as Devon has an above average age profile) may be the top of the list for action in that locality. The list of national priorities, district priorities and that of the local patient may well not match comfortably. An approach that looks to see where these can all be accommodated and to respond as well as possible will give a purpose to the process of locality planning.

Locality priorities

The wealth of information from the sources outlined above will inform the strategy and the next step will be to determine the priority areas for action. An example of how this might be done is shown in Figure 6.3. The locality health strategy can plot the milestones of achievement, plan for a service development by looking beyond an annual cycle and design the short steps to arrive at the desired outcome. Achieving consensus on priority areas with the many players involved in the process will need to be guided by the principles outlined in earlier chapters. Achieving priorities should be an iterative process where reality about what is achievable and affordable guides the discussion. In summary the questions that must be asked should be:

- Is this an effective service?
- Is this efficiently delivered?
- Is this going to improve the quality of life for our patients?
- Is this service offering value for money?
- Is this service acceptable to service users?
- Is this service based on best clinical evidence?

All sorts of models of priority assessing have been established looking at issues such as volume ratios, costs, years of quality life gained etc., etc. The most pragmatic answer is that making choices about locality priorities is likely to be developed more from a basis of affordability than any other. However, further help is at hand with the increasing stress placed on looking at services through audit, evaluation, research and effectiveness studies. The aim is for services to be evaluated on evidence not just opinion! This can be most appropriately done by locality based audits both in primary care or jointly commissioned and also by those provided by trusts and other providers. It is essential that LCGs do not re-invent the wheel but have access to the range of data that is already available that will give information as well as frameworks to develop local reviews. Using sources of information from national studies, randomized control trials and other databases to assess the experience of a locality will help to inform the priorities and plan the actions.

	MEDIUM-TERM STRATEGY		PREVENTIVE CARE	
STRATEGY	REASON FOR CHANGE	TARGET GROUP	WORK TO BE DONE	EXPECTED ACHIEVEMENTS
STROKE	• High rate in some Mid-Devon wards	• All groups and smokers and people with raised blood pressure	• Continue to support Stop Smoking initiatives through multi-agency forum • Offer support for healthier lifestyles through 'helping people change' and 'health script' • Raise awareness of importance of BP checks, physical activity, avoiding obesity • Encourage sensible levels of alcohol, salt intake	• Increase in number of smokers who stop • Increased levels of activity in people referred • Increased knowledge of risk factors
		• Patients over 65 years with risk factors or stroke previously	• Appropriate prescribing practice • Investigation of prescribing rates for anti-hypertensive drugs • Participation in integrated stroke care project	• Improved outcome for patients with stroke
BREAST CANCER	• Large variation across locality – higher rates in Cullompton/Crediton	• Women in 50+ age group	• Encourage attendance at routine screening programme, targeting poor attenders • Age of death from cancer audit • Follow-up primary care audit and admission rates • Use findings to develop educational programme if appropriate	• Discover reason for variation and implement measures to reduce it

Figure 6.3: An excerpt from the medium-term strategy section (preventative care) of a locality health strategy.

Action plans and medium-term strategies

A locality health strategy will need to decide on some immediate actions to address the priorities that have been agreed. An example of such an action plan, which may come at the end of a locality health strategy, is shown in Figure 6.4.

This not only gives momentum to locality commissioning but encourages the contributors – practices, agencies and users – to see that their contribution has been valued and that steps have been taken to respond to it. Too often purchasing plans have been seen as remote, lacking immediate impact and rather vague in their deliveries of priorities. An action plan needs to have some timescales attached, identify who is going to be responsible for seeing it through and most importantly for reporting back on achievements and outcomes at a later date. Locality commissioning must be seen to deliver. All the strategies in the world will not change anything unless there are positive results.

Some issues are not possible to fix quickly and a more measured approach will be needed. This may be because of affordability or because services need to change internally and adjustments take time. Restraint on how contracts can be moved from one provider to another or services withdrawn or changed will need to be developed over time and also to meet statutory requirements for giving notice. The prevention of ill health due to such things as smoking, poor diet or lack of exercise can be tackled in a variety of ways but the effects of change will be very long term.

A locality health strategy's primary purpose is to encapsulate the variety of needs in an area and understand what is required to address them. The strategy gives an opportunity for all the participants to look at the whole picture of health, at their part in the process and provide a considered review of the future direction of commissioning services.

Spreading the news

The process of drawing up a locality health strategy by engaging and then summarizing all the influences that have contributed to it will be an important part of the ownership of the final document. Having achieved a strategy this will then provide further opportunities for discussion by presenting the findings to a variety of fora in the district. It will be a long time before the local population or even other professionals fully understand the implications of locality commissioning but the distribution of LCG annual reports and locality health strategies throughout surgeries, libraries and other places is a start. The inevitable local media interest can be used to explain the process of locality commissioning, the nature of changes envisaged and to develop a sense of local corporate ownership of health strategy. As far as the GPs themselves are concerned, LCGs or their executives will meet collectively on a regular basis but visits to individual practices and participation in a debate about how the strategy is being used will reinforce the role and contribution by the practice. Quite often the process is as important as the outcome itself.

Planning at district level

It is likely that locality groups will increasingly take on many of the functions of a previously centralized DHA. All the same a coherent overall planning strategy will still require that a number of services are commissioned at health authority level. The relevant services are likely to be those which are highly specialist in nature (e.g. rare cancers), those where there is high cost but low volume (e.g. forensic services), those where there is no local service (e.g. cardiac surgery), specialist emergency services (e.g. special care baby units or ITU) or those services which involve complex tertiary referrals (e.g. mental health, learning disability or physically disabled people with exceptional needs).

As LCGs take on increased work, health authorities are likely to merge and become 'super health authorities' and therefore relatively remote from their large populations. The need for LCGs to co-ordinate successfully with each other and with the central health authority will become all the greater. The structure for such planning at DHA level is likely to be along the lines of Figures 4.5 and 4.6 (*see* Chapter 4 – creating a structure). Within this structure, representatives of LCGs and the locality management teams from a whole district can meet with each other and also with the health authority to make plans on district issues. This commissioning board will be responsible for any decisions on commissioning and prioritization, that need to be made at district level and for integrating these district commissioning plans with the locality plans of individual groups. It is likely that individual LCGs (rather than the whole board) will be able to lead on some service development issues and share their work with other groups in the district and also with the commissioning board of the health authority. This might be possible with services such as community based specialist nurses, specialist palliative care services and complex care services. In this way work can be delegated and shared out appropriately between LCGs while the commissioning board can maintain the final say. The alternative might be for lead GPs to be given executive positions on the main health authority board but this could lead to theoretical problems around the health authority's role as purchaser.

ACTION PLAN 1997/98 – SUMMARY	PREVENTIVE CARE
MID-DEVON LOCALITY ACTION	**IN PARTNERSHIP WITH ...**
• Carry out Audit of Health Script Scheme at Culm Vale Leisure Centre	Mid-Devon District Council and Centre Manager
• Disseminate and develop follow-up work to Health of the Nation seminar in West Devon	West Devon Borough Council and South & West Devon Health Authority
• Pilot scheme in Mid-Devon to enable Primary Health Care Team member to refer patients for advice on environmental factors which may be affecting their health	Mid-Devon District Council and Primary Health Care Team
• Develop survey methodology and carry out survey of accident experience, preventative measures in place and risk perception of accidents in Crediton area	Devon County Council Road Safety Unit, Locality Planning Team
• Identify households without a smoke alarm where small children are resident and provide one free of charge	Health Visitors, Devon Fire & Rescue Service, South West Water
• Develop oral health training programme for Health Visitors and School Nurses and provide training day and resources	Exeter & District Community Health Services NHS Trust, Northern Devon Healthcare Trust and the Community Dental Service

ACTION PLAN 1997/98 – SUMMARY	PRIMARY CARE
MID-DEVON LOCALITY ACTION	**IN PARTNERSHIP WITH ...**
• Develop Locality Commissioning to ensure all GP practices are involved in purchasing decisions	Mid-Devon GP practices
• Establish a Practice Manager's network to contribute to commissioning policy	Mid-Devon GP practices
• Investigate methods of developing primary care to raise standards through accreditation, peer support and educational programmes	Mid-Devon GP practices and Primary Health Care Team
• Participate in a review of Practice Reports with a view to making these more useful to practices and more informative about future developments	Mid-Devon GP practices
• Extend information about Mid-Devon Doctors Commissioning Group via Newsletter and Annual Report and encourage links with Community Health Council and other groups	Mid-Devon GP practices, CHC and local user groups
• Liaise with Out of Hours Co-ordinator and continue to look for improved solutions in Mid-Devon	Mid-Devon GP practices and Devon doctors
• Investigate prescribing rates of anti-hypertensive drugs	Prescribing Adviser and Mid-Devon GP practices
• Review case history of premature deaths from breast cancer	Selected practices in Mid-Devon and Primary Care Audit Team
• Keep under review the availability of NHS Dentistry and encourage dentists into the area's hotspots, particularly in West Devon	Dental Advisory Group
• Participation in the integrated care projects for stroke management and care of diabetic foot	Primary Care Audit Team, Mid-Devon Primary Care Team and NHS Trusts
• Participate in district-wide diabetic audit	Primary Care Audit Team, Mid-Devon Primary Care Team and NHS Trusts

Figure 6.4: A sample action plan taken from a locality health strategy. (*Continued overleaf.*)

ACTION PLAN 1997/98 – SUMMARY	SERVICES IN THE COMMUNITY
MID-DEVON LOCALITY ACTION	**IN PARTNERSHIP WITH ...**
• Seek to extend the contract with Relate following year-end audit and consider other options for counselling services	Crediton GP practices, Relate and Social Services
• To contribute to the Joint Consultative Committees as they become established and to agree priorities and Joint Finance Schemes with Housing and Social Services that meet local priorities	West Devon Borough Council, Mid-Devon District Council and Devon County Council
• Following the agreement of a specification for community nursing, negotiate 24-hour access to district nursing	Exeter & District Community Health Service NHS Trust and Mid-Devon GPs
• Audit the Reablement Phase II development in Tiverton/Cullompton and consider Okehampton's needs for a reablement approach	Exeter & District Community Health Service NHS Trust and Social Services
• Together with Social Services and local users, develop a register and map of dementia services to prepare for Joint Purchasing Protocol	Mid-Devon Social Services and Exeter & District Community Health Services NHS Trust
• Discuss with GPs a process to design a specification for palliative care and terminal care services that meets the expectations for a range of support services	Mid-Devon GPs, Exeter & District Community Health Service NHS Trust, Royal Devon & Exeter Hospital and Marie Curie
• Negotiate services to be purchased from a re-provided Tiverton Hospital in preparation for a detailed business plan	Exeter & District Community Health Service NHS Trust and Mid-Devon GPs

ACTION PLAN 1997/98 – SUMMARY	HOSPITAL SERVICES
MID-DEVON LOCALITY ACTION	**IN PARTNERSHIP WITH ...**
• Develop role of community hospitals to accept medical admissions transferred from the Royal Devon & Exeter Hospital as priority cases	Exeter & District Community Health Services NHS Trust and Royal Devon & Exeter Healthcare NHS Trust
• Monitor compliance with service standards in ENT, ophthalmology, orthopaedics and draw up specification for the services	Royal Devon & Exeter Healthcare NHS Trust and Mid-Devon GPs
• Set standards for cancellations of outpatient clinics and monitor performance. Devise project to reduce number of patients who do not attend	Royal Devon & Exeter Healthcare NHS Trust and Mid-Devon GPs
• Identify savings from reduced Extra Contractual Referrals and develop local services	Mid-Devon GPs and NHS Trusts
• Monitor ambulance exception reports for Mid-Devon	Westcountry Ambulance Services NHS Trust and rural GP practices

Figure 6.4: *continued.*

These district issues are likely to be of less interest to individual GPs in a locality than more directly local issues. The lead GPs or locality medical directors will, nevertheless, need to keep their LCGs informed of any planning decisions at district level and consult directly with any member GPs, who may have a special interest in any specific issues.

Planning with trusts and specialists

Trusts need to plan their future services and consultants need to develop their specialties. Two main logistic problems hamper joint planning between purchasers and providers. Firstly, one LCG may deal with several trusts and vice versa. Secondly, in an ideal world, all trusts in a locality would produce a coherent planning strategy that ran parallel to that of the health authority and its LCGs but this is made difficult when local trusts are in competition with each other. Collaboration between trusts rather than competition is now being sought and it is to be hoped in the future that this will develop to avoid waste, duplication of services, excessive bureaucracy and expensive invoicing and contracting processes.

The first problem is illustrated in Figure 6.5 (i) and shows the ideal planning situation with one health authority, one trust and two LCGs. Each of the LCGs can individually discuss short-term planning and strategic purchasing issues with the trust along the lines discussed in the next chapter. Decisions in these areas can then give way to longer term commitments between the trust and the LCG concerning what is appropriate for the patients of that locality. Planning issues between the trusts and the LCGs that cannot be decided at locality level can then be deferred to district level. There the DHA, the two LCGs and the trust can collaboratively make long-term district-wide planning decisions that can provide the trust with both direction and stability. Though ideal from the planning point of view, with only one trust there is no competition and, therefore, no purchasing leverage as far as the LCGs and the purchasing health authority are concerned. The dual roles of planning and purchasing are, therefore, very much in opposition as the ideal planning situation is the reverse of the ideal purchasing situation and vice versa. This is being increasingly recognized as all stakeholders are now being encouraged to collaborate especially where there is a monopoly provider. In reality the relationship between the DHA, trusts and LCGs is more likely to be represented in Figures 6.5 (ii) and 6.5 (iii).

Figure 6.5 (ii) depicts the situation when there is a large commissioning group, which is responsible for a large part of the population covered by its present health authority. Such a commissioning group is likely to have

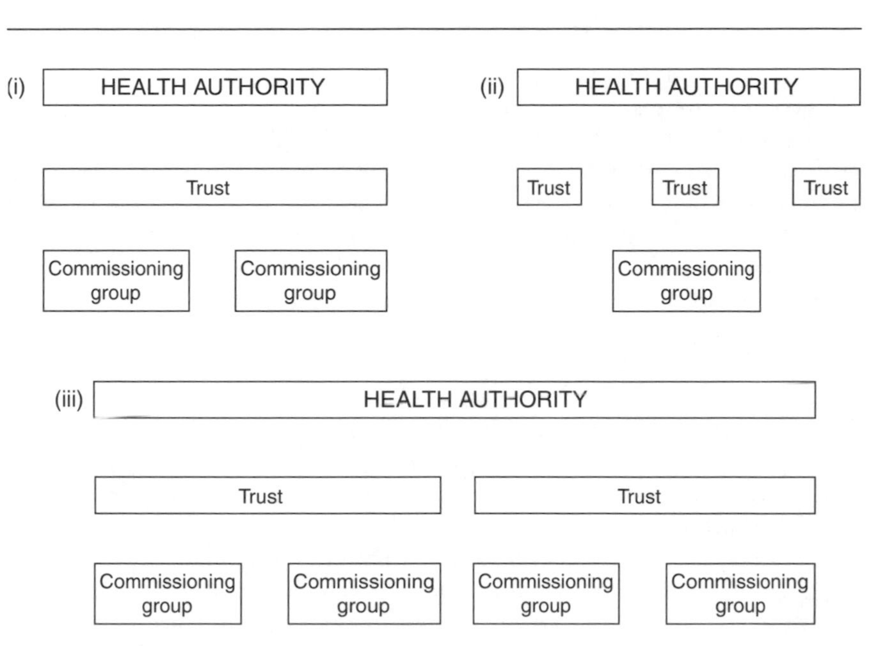

Figure 6.5: Models showing the interrelationships between a health authority, local trusts and its constituent commissioning groups.

its services provided by several trusts, which from a strategic purchasing angle might offer the group potentially increased choice in purchasing leverage. However, from the planning point of view there may be unnecessary duplication and poor co-ordination of services throughout the geographical area. Ideally such a commissioning group might want to involve all local trusts in planning discussions but this might be difficult given the present competitive nature of the relationship between trusts. LCGs in Warwickshire, Enfield and Haringey have overcome this problem by meeting with all local consultants representing a particular specialty from different trusts resulting in coherent strategies that both sides can sign up to. Likewise the Northants and East Dorset Commissioning Groups have established specialty liaison groups, which in Dorset meet with the clinicians of all three local NHS trusts. They are simply trying to balance the dichotomy between purchasing and planning. In time it is conceivable that consultants will attend such meetings with their managers (rather than vice versa!) and it will become clearer where collaborative working and competition begin and end. Large long-term developments, which require considerable investment, will probably continue to be decided at health authority level and possibly without regional input as the health authorities enlarge (and the regional tier begins to disappear). In all such decisions the relevant LCGs and trusts will clearly need to be involved.

Figure 6.5 (iii) depicts the situation with medium-sized GP commissioning groups, where each is dealing with more than one trust and where each trust is needing to deal with a number of LCGs. Short-term planning and strategic purchasing issues that are relevant to the locality can once again be accomplished by direct meetings between each LCG and each trust, as described in the next chapter. For major developments a trust will require a coherent planning lead from all the LCGs that it deals with. This will require close liaison between the relevant LCGs and one way of undertaking this work (which occurs in North and East Devon) is for each LCG to lead on specified issues agreed collectively by all the groups. This means that in North and East Devon where there are four LCGs, each group only has to do a quarter of the work that it would otherwise have to do on its own and the trust and consultants only have to meet with one group rather than four. Planning work and decisions can then be shared with all the groups. Within each locality there may be minor adaptations to the basic strategy to meet local needs and at the other end of the spectrum there will be some major developmental decisions that will still need to be made at health authority level in order to take in the wider picture beyond the localities.

Towards integrated planning

LCGs, health authorities and trusts will need to agree at which level different sorts of planning decisions are to be made. The majority of decisions, as we have seen, can be made and integrated at locality level. These might include major decisions such as the planning and reprovision of a large community hospital within a locality. Outside the locality, LCGs still have an important role to play in allowing trusts to plan ahead in a rather more stable environment than we have seen in recent years. Finally, LCGs can be the medium whereby the local population and its primary care team can influence planning decisions at district level and thereby ensure that such decisions have grass roots approval. In short, locality commissioning offers an integrated service: integrated services at locality level, integration between locality and district planning decisions and integration of primary and secondary services that are clinically led by GPs and specialists. Collaboration and not competition must drive the process as the available resources are too scarce to waste. This is why many are welcoming the steps taken by the present government, which will see the replacement of the internal market with a more collaborative and partnership oriented approach but one which will retain an important aspect of planning and accountancy for services available.

7 Involvement in purchasing

This chapter is called 'involvement in purchasing' rather than simply 'purchasing' for good reason. That is to say LCGs are not themselves the purchasers but rather their health authorities who are. Neither do they hold budgets – again this is the responsibility of their health authority. Nevertheless in a market system that implies winners and losers, several groups have wanted to become involved in purchasing in order to prevent their patients from becoming the losers. One distinguishing aspect of such involvement, however, is that any improvements in trust services that result are available to all patients, GPs and LCGs – there are no losers. Though groups have been able to make a substantial impact within the internal market, everything described in this chapter could continue in its absence. All that LCGs require in the future is a division of responsibility between those who assess the need and allocate resources and those who provide the care.

Caveats aside, many LCGs have wanted to have some involvement in purchasing as a means of fine tuning their commissioning decisions and guiding them to fruition. A purchasing interest offers groups access to the 'how' rather than the 'what' questions about services that are to be provided. With all groups, any such involvement is co-operative with the local health authority and extends only to strategic purchasing decisions, while operational decisions are left to the health authority itself.

At the very beginning, each group will need to establish with the health authority its own 'modus operandi' in becoming involved in such strategic purchasing decisions. This will include the degree to which the group wishes to participate and co-operate in this process, the priority areas for such activity and its criteria for new, improved or altered services.

How involved does the group wish to be in the purchasing process?

Each group will need to decide how it wishes to participate in purchasing decisions. Many groups provide mainly advisory input. Some are more closely involved. Increasingly, as we have seen, health authorities are putting in place structures so that group executives or lead GPs can directly engage in purchasing decisions with purchasing boards or special subcommittees of the health authority. The establishment by health authorities of locality management teams with locality purchasers allows a further degree of co-operative involvement in the purchasing process. Where health authorities provide such teams with notional budgets, this potentially allows LCGs to share responsibility with the health authority in how the money is spent. Whatever the level of engagement, it is imperative that this is decided by the LCG itself and by no one else.

In what purchasing areas does the group wish to be involved?

Each locality group will need to decide in what areas intervention is likely to be effective. The views of individual GPs can be sought either at locality meetings of the whole group or via locality representatives. Questionnaires can be useful and telephoning to confirm problem areas can engender a sense of group commitment. Some groups have special service alert forms, sometimes called 'yellow cards', which signal up areas where GPs are finding problems with local trusts. Invariably there will be some issues that are common to many LCGs, for example the desire for open access investigation and some issues which are common to most GPs in the locality because the local trust is particularly poor at providing these. For many groups priority areas will have been identified within the locality health strategy (*see* Chapter 6).

What are the locality group's purchasing criteria for a service?

Each group will need to establish its own purchasing criteria but the questions itemized below are likely to be relevant.

(i) *Does it serve a local need?* If GPs are raising an issue then it is likely to. This may need confirmation by a number of routes. Public health involvement in the locality may indicate that the need is there (*see* Chapter 5).

(ii) *Do the local population want it?* However laudable a service is – if it is not wanted and if it is therefore not going to be used by the local population then it is clearly being inappropriately purchased. If the group has a public accountability structure (*see* Chapter 9) then it can check with its local population that there is a genuine wish for such a service.

(iii) *Is it clinically effective?* Reading the literature and possible involvement of public health and the primary care audit group may be appropriate (*see* Chapter 8). Many audit groups are beginning to encourage the critical appraisement of evidence via CASP workshops in localities. LCGs may be able to use such workshops and organize meetings where there is an appropriate mix of local health professionals who can review the relevant evidence for a particular service.

(iv) *Is the service safe and appropriate?* If a new service is to be purchased in a community hospital, for instance, it may seem desirable to have a local service but safety factors and consultation with specialists may indicate that a service would be better sited centrally. There will always be limitations on what can be achieved in a local centre in terms of the equipment and staff available.

(v) *Is the proposal cost-effective?* It may, for instance, seem appropriate to have open access ultrasound at a community hospital but its level of use may not justify the expense of siting it peripherally.

(vi) *Does the proposal conflict with national planning and priority guidelines?* Health authorities are required to meet national planning and priority guidelines from central government. Clearly they and the LCG need to adhere to best professional practice and this may require them to seek the advice of professional bodies. The Calman report, for example, specifies national guidelines on the provision of cancer services in selected units and cancer centres.

Purchasing options and approaches

On the face of it a free market offers only one purchasing option. If you do not like the services of one provider then purchase from another. In practice such 'spot purchasing' has had a minimum impact on the NHS even within the fundholding model. Effective involvement in purchasing by LCGs puts the emphasis on co-operation and integration rather than market forces.

Purchasing new services

LCGs have been successfully involved in purchasing new services using new (development) money and have sometimes been able to develop a new service at no extra cost. Experience from many groups has shown that various stages are necessary to do this successfully.

(i) Do your homework and ensure that the service to be purchased fits within the purchasing criteria of your LCG (see above).

(ii) Do a preliminary sounding with the health authority to see if this fits the strategic direction of the authority purchasing plans.

(iii) Discuss the proposals, preferably face to face, with all those involved. For instance, if an LCG is asking for open access echocardiography then it needs to involve cardiologists, technicians and trust managers. The result of these discussions may lead to changes in the proposal concerning issues such as relevant criteria for referral, relevant training of GPs to use such investigations and involvement of specialists.

(iv) Draw up a specification and a protocol for the new proposed service and identify how it will be audited.

(v) Secure funding and resources with the health authority. Ensure that the proposal is in the health authority's strategic plan and that the money is identified for implementation in a future contract.

(vi) Agree a timescale and liaise with all relevant participants.

This kind of process has led to a large number of innovative developments that have been catalysed by LCGs. Box 7.1 provides examples of some of these projects which may be helpful for other LCGs who are thinking of purchasing new services themselves.

Box 7.1: Examples of projects that have been introduced by LCGs

New service	Commissioning group
Acute back scheme	Nottingham, Brighton and Hove
Locality back pain clinic manned by clinical assistant	East Dorset
Fast track orthopaedic service for working patients who are off work as a result of an orthopaedic injury	East Dorset
Teenage health promotion clinics	East Dorset
Open access echocardiography	Small Heath Project, Blackpool, Wyre and Fylde, Brent
Fast track exercise ECG	Small Heath Project, Brent
Open access EEG	North West Bristol
24-hr ECG and BP monitoring	Brent
Direct access oesophagogastroscopy	Brent
Post-myocardial rehabilitation programme	Blackpool, Wyre and Fylde
Out-reach anticoagulant service	Blackpool, Wyre and Fylde
Fast track angina clinic	Small Heath Project
Acute investigation of possible DVT	Mid-Devon
Direct access same day ultrasound for threatened miscarriage	Northamptonshire
Direct access to the tonsillectomy waiting list	Northamptonshire
One stop neurology clinic for headaches	East Dorset

continued overleaf

Box 7.1: *continued*

New service	**Commissioning group**
Acute medical admissions to local nursing homes rather than district general hospital	Huddersfield, Mid-Devon
24-hr community nursing	Lothian
GP access to nurses for male catheterization	Small Heath Project
GP access to named social worker	Small Heath Project
Practice-based and operated cryotherapy for warts	Harrow
Primary care-based epilepsy service	North West Bristol

Improving services that are already being purchased from a local trust

The reality, however, is that new money for new services will become increasingly thin on the ground. The challenge and the main role of the LCG in purchasing will not be to move services from trust to trust but to improve services that the health authority is already purchasing. The sheer size of an LCG should lend it immense weight in changing local trust services for the better. Many LCGs are involved in re-specifying contracts and with responsive trusts many are seeing improved services as a result. The key is a willingness on the part of all sides (GPs, health authority, trust and consultants) to discuss and agree on relevant issues and a motivation to improve things.

Some trusts and some specialties within other trusts are less responsive and when this happens the LCG may need to assert itself as a representative purchaser as well as the negotiator of improved services. A mechanism for doing so will be outlined which does not require the LCG to be a direct purchaser though it does require the health authority to change its purchasing activity if the specifications of the LCG are not met. The stages in this process are listed below.

Establish a purchasing mechanism

The health authority has to be able to switch a contract from one provider to another if it is to have any weight as a purchaser. In practice, health authorities are frequently unwilling, and even unable, to switch contracts because the loss of a large contract with a provider may lead to the closure of a whole department or even a whole trust. Alternatively a trust may simply respond by putting up the unit costs of the remaining contracts with the health authority and the latter ends up effectively paying for services that it is no longer using. Similarly, if another purchaser pulls out of a substantial contract the impact on the remaining purchasers can be immense as there will be less sharing of fixed overheads thus forcing up costs to others. Consequently changing contracts has to be an option of last resort. Signalling longer-term changes in purchasing should ideally be a shared debate with local providers with longer timescales to effect necessary service changes. Service agreements will give notice of a necessity to change before the ultimate threat of withdrawal. Nevertheless, if the health authority is to have any purchasing power it must as a last resort have a theoretical ability to change provider and needs to draw up a set of guidelines for doing this. Box 7.2 demonstrates how this might be done in practice.

Box 7.2: Withdrawal of service agreements

1 The authority must have the ability to withdraw contracts from one provider and place them with another, if it is to be effective as a purchaser.

2 The authority recognizes that providers will need to be able to plan ahead to achieve down-sizing and, therefore, the following approach is proposed:

Contract value <£100k	6 months from notice	Reduction at full cost
Contract value <£500k	6 months from notice:	Reduction at marginal cost
	12 months from notice:	Reduction at full cost
Contract value >£500k	6 months from notice:	Reduction at marginal cost
but <£2500k	24 months from notice:	Reduction at full cost
Contract value >£2500k	To be negotiated	

In such a system small amounts of money can be removed from a trust at short notice while large amounts of money require much longer terms of notice. With the move towards three-year contracts the details of such an arrangement may change but the principle will still hold.

Establish which contracts you are going to focus on

The particular contracts or specialties concerned are often obvious to an LCG but impressions should be confirmed by meetings or personal communication with locality GPs and their representatives. It is particularly important to establish at this early stage that locality GPs are concerned enough about the quality of a service to commit themselves to switching to an alternative provider if everything fails.

Establish your bargaining position

In order to establish its initial position, an LCG must decide with its member GPs what are its minimum standards for continuation of a contract and what are its optimal standards. It is essential to commit these to paper and to circulate them to the health authority and to the relevant trust so that they are pre-warned of the locality group's dissatisfaction. They should also be given the evidence of audits to demonstrate the relevant difficulties. Proposals for change should also be made clear at this stage.

Meet with all the stakeholders

The lead GPs or executive of an LCG will now need to meet with the health authority, the trust and with the consultants. If the commissioning group's structure allows it, it may be ideal to meet with all three at the same time. The crucial meeting is now between the representative GPs and the consultants of the specialty concerned. Here the GPs can explain why they are concerned and consultants can explain their problems and what they feel they can deliver. The meeting of the two sides is important because if they can agree then both are thereby committed to the result. An agreement that suits all sides is the norm. The synchronous presence of managers is important not only to witness and minute decisions but to respond when the forces against change are coming not from the doctors but from the health authority or the trust itself. The final aim of the meeting must be to produce a service specification (an example is given in Box 7.3) which needs to itemize exactly the expectations on both sides on all the issues discussed. These should be circulated to all parties to confirm what has been agreed. Specifications can vary from a detailed description

Box 7.3: Service specification sheet (example)

1 Waiting times
   (a) Maximum non-acute outpatient waiting time (e.g. 12 weeks)
   (b) Maximum non-acute waiting time for operation (e.g. 9 months)
   (c) Arrangements for urgent appointments and operations

2 Correspondence
   (a) Time taken for patients to receive notice of an appointment (e.g. 2 weeks)
   (b) Time taken for GP to receive outpatient letter (e.g. 1 week)
   (c) Time taken for GP to receive discharge report (e.g. 1 week)

3 Communication
   (a) Arrangements for direct communication with consultants
   (b) Arrangements for non-urgent communication with consultants
   (c) How results of major investigations are communicated to patients

4 Referral guidelines
   (a) Referral procedure and criteria for common conditions

5 Audit
   Mutually acceptable means of auditing that service specifications have been met with a 6-month period prior to reviewing contracts for 1997/98

of the nature of the proposed service to a fairly simple service standards sheet. The amount of detail necessary will depend on the nature of the problem. If it is at all likely that a contract might be switched from one provider to another then this would involve a comprehensive specification.

Publish purchasing intentions with relevant period of notice prior to possible change of contract

Having decided on mutually agreed service specifications, an LCG needs to clarify the length of time that it is allowing before these standards must be met. Specifications and the relevant timescale must then be published for all to see. The locality health strategy should include the expected arrangements for monitoring and if there is likely to be a change of providers then this will need to be specified.

Agree arrangements for auditing trust performance

It is important to specify the nature of any audits that will be done, when they will be done, who will do them and what criteria are being set. Such audits do not commit either purchaser or provider to any particular course of action but do mean that they are able to specify the level of service quality at any one time compared to that at a later date. Where a trust is put on notice for a particular contract it is vital that an LCG specifies exactly when it is going to perform the audit that will decide whether the trust continues to get the full contract or not. Most trusts will aim to get their service 'up to scratch' well before this audit date both as a means of ensuring that they meet the specifications without difficulty and also to show that they are committed to the improvements that have been agreed.

In many cases it may be quite unnecessary to invoke the purchasing mechanism at all in such negotiations. Where a trust is particularly unresponsive it may be necessary on occasion to put a contract on notice prior to meeting with the trust and the consultants. It may seem an aggressive way for an LCG to operate but is in fact a far more conciliatory use of the market mechanism than has been previously employed by fundholders or total purchasers. For health authorities it offers them an effective way of bringing trust services up to scratch when they have been unable to do this on their own. It is a fact of life that sometimes an LCG may need to put a poorly performing service on notice simply to announce its presence and give notice to the trust that it means business. The views of a trust director who has been through this process are illustrated in Box 7.4.

Undoubtedly the purchaser has the upper hand when he or she is well resourced. Unfortunately, one of the effects of improving waiting times is to increase throughout and even a well-resourced health authority can rapidly run out of funds. As shortages become widespread throughout the NHS, LCGs are having to negotiate from a position where money is short and, given that a health authority is not allowed to go over budget, this undermines its negotiating strength. To quote the same trust director in Box 7.4, 'The ability of the group to influence waiting times must be limited when resources in its host Health Authority are scarce. However, the groups have a very definite role to play in examining referral patterns and working with consultants to ensure appropriate referrals, which may, in some cases, lead to an improvement in waiting times through a reduction in demand'. He adds rather pessimistically 'This is pure theory at

Box 7.4: The hospital trust view – dealing with LCGs

(Steven Jupp, Director of Personnel & Contracting, Royal Devon & Exeter Healthcare NHS Trust)

'The basis of any effective relationship is a high degree of trust between the parties. If such an environment can be created, difficult and challenging agendas can often be managed and the result should mean better services for patients and better relationships between hospital doctors and GPs.

It is always possible to try to bring about change by means of threat and "purchasing" power, but it is generally accepted that such change, if achieved, usually brings soured relationships, resentment and the "victim" waiting to take revenge! However, because of the trust already built up between the group and the hospital, it was possible for the relationship to survive and flourish when the group (through the Health Authority's Purchasing Intentions) gave notice that, unless improvements were brought about within an agreed timescale, 20% of the contract for that speciality would be withdrawn the following year. This caused considerable concern amongst some staff in the Trust. However, after calm consideration, the frustrations of the GPs were recognised and work was started to address the difficulties. A statement such as this from outside an organisation can provide a helpful impetus to change which is already recognised as necessary.

For some time the group had been concerned about a number of service issues in one particular speciality:

- waiting times
- timeliness of response to GPs' letters
- difficult communications between consultants and GPs
- referral guidance
- not knowing who to contact with concerns.

continued overleaf

Box 7.4: *continued*

As a result we clarified our management arrangement so that the group was quite clear as to who was accountable for delivering service changes. We were then able to facilitate the development of a service specification which contained a number of quality standards concerning communications and timeliness of the service. It was crucial that these were agreed between consultants and GPs.

In order to ensure change was effective and sustained, the Trust participated in an audit which showed that substantial progress had been made, with improvements in all areas of concern. As a result the notice was withdrawn and the contracting arrangements were settled. The Trust Director concerned noted that it was *crucial* that specifications were agreed between consultants and GPs. With the Health Authority it was equally crucial to have GPs involved and not only because they can flag up what changes are necessary and can sign up their group to these changes. GPs have to be pragmatists and they are able to debate issues with Trust managers and specialists, who may have a myopic or purist view of what is necessary or practical. They can also commit consultants and their own locality GPs to a course of action which managers, on their own, would find very difficult'.

the moment as our experience to date is that no specialty has experienced a significant decrease in referral rates over recent years'. Consequently, LCGs and trusts are now beginning to look at how they can get more from the same pot of money. This is a form of involvement that tends to require more in terms of goodwill, commitment, motivation and co-operation and less in terms of the LCG being a representative of its health authority as purchaser.

Getting more services for your money

In future, the emphasis in the NHS is likely to move away from costs *per se* towards providing quality and efficiency within an established network of prices and costs. It will, therefore, be an increasing challenge for GPs, consultants and trusts to meet and redefine each service within the existing cash envelope. Some of these meetings may become more doctor to doctor than purchaser to provider as described above but the locality group will still be defined to some extent by its relationship with the health authority as purchaser. So what can GPs, consultants and trusts do to make the pot of money for a particular service go further? Some of the issues that LCGs have looked at are listed below.

Cancellations

Patients cancel or fail to turn up for appointments and consultants cancel clinics because of unpredicted study leave or holiday. Both are worth auditing. If the number of cancellations or DNAs by patients is large then there are a number of ways of improving things – altering the timing of appointments being sent out, asking patients to confirm appointments, GPs dictating referral letters in front of them, etc. Conversely, if a large proportion of consultant clinics are being cancelled then the trust needs to forward plan, e.g. allow for times when several consultants are likely to be on annual leave. The maximum percentage of cancelled clinics can be entered in a contract specification.

Follow-ups

Some specialties follow-up patients more than others and where follow-ups are unnecessary the available space could be used for seeing new patients. An audit of follow-ups by an LCG can look at whether they were necessary and whether useful information was obtained in the outpatient letter and thereby determine if there is a problem. If there is, this might suggest the need for a meeting of GPs and consultants.

Extra contractual referrals

These usually provide a little fat that can be used to increase resources for a particular local service. LCGs have shown that they can reduce GP referrals simply by notifying all GPs where contracts are presently held, identifying the more expensive ones and applying mild peer pressure. Sometimes, local services will be unable to cope with referrals that were previously sent outside the district. In such cases, the treatment of anorexia nervosa for instance, the locality or district may need to invest in a local service provided that it can be shown to be more cost effective than the service that was previously provided outside the district. One option is for an LCG to appoint a lead GP as 'ombudsman' to arbitrate over extra contractual referrals, which are being questioned by the health authority.

If GPs are to sign up to this then health authorities should ensure that some of the savings can be reinvested in services for the locality.

An LCG can also be instrumental in reducing consultant extra contractual referrals. For instance, an audit of consultant extra contractual referrals may show that these are spread arbitrarily among a large number of units especially where several consultants are concerned. Money can be saved for the local service by having fewer and larger volume contracts and often without affecting the standard of service provided.

Benchmarking

Benchmarking is a useful way of assessing local trust performance by comparing this with what is offered elsewhere. It is important that benchmarks are established which compare like with like (e.g. community vs community – acute vs acute – South East vs South East, etc., etc.). The emphasis hitherto has been on price but future benchmarking is likely to place the emphasis on activity, clinical outcomes, quality and efficiency.

There may be a significant discrepancy in prices for a similar procedure between one hospital trust and another and also frequently between the same procedure being done by a hospital trust or a community trust (e.g. minor operations). Some of these discrepancies frequently appear to be due to rather arbitrary price fixing, which may have been inevitable given the speed with which the internal market was introduced. Some of these differences in prices may also reflect marketing strategy by a local trust wanting to be competitive in some areas and the feeling that it does not need to be in others. In theory, this should not happen because of the 'price must equal cost' rule but in practice it probably does. Nevertheless, some of the differences in costs may be related to straightforward efficiency, economies of scale, the different capital charges, different working practices, etc.... and in these cases the price differences between one trust and another will be to some extent 'real'. As LCGs develop their purchasing role they will want to start looking at those areas where their local trust seems to be more expensive than others and will need to find out why this is so. Once the reasons are known then both the LCG and the trust have the option of either changing the relevant service to bring it in line with perceived average costs or keeping the service as it is because it offers something that the cheaper options do not. Using this method of benchmarking, the LCG will also find out if a trust is passing on increased costs from one specialty to another or possibly favouring one sort of purchaser (e.g. a cost per case fundholder) against another (e.g. a cost and volume health authority purchaser). So far the market system and the rules that govern it have favoured the fundholder purchasing at the margins but in future the larger bulk purchaser (e.g. an LCG) should become the favoured customer. This will only be so if the LCGs can show themselves to be as 'keen' purchasers as the individual fundholders. Benchmarking will become an easier and more accurate undertaking when and if purchasers are all purchasing in the same way (e.g. cost and volume) and to the same timescale (e.g. three-yearly contracts). In the absence of an internal market, LCGs and the health authorities will need to develop systems of benchmarking that concentrate on performance rather than cost.

Analysing referrals

An LCG clearly has no right to interfere with the referrals of its individual GPs without their blessing. Nevertheless, some referrals are more necessary than others and audit, education and peer review can free-up the referral system so that more appointments are available for the patients that need them, waiting times are reduced and the referral system becomes generally more cost effective. Referrals can be analysed in a number of ways though a great deal of trust within an LCG is necessary for this to occur. Individual practices or indeed individual partners can be compared according to rates of referral and the information can catalyse change. Initially an individual GP or practice might benefit from seeing their position on a scatter chart with anonymous data from other GPs and practices within a locality. At a later stage the doctors in the locality may feel able to share information more freely.

The group may be able to agree on 'quality indicators,' e.g. the percentage of surgical patients who are operated on, etc. If reducing referrals means that more work has to be done in primary care then this must be recognized financially though it is still likely to be cheaper than using specialist services. Some LCGs are looking at 'referral guidelines', which specify the sorts of patients that do and do not need referring and what GPs can do for those that do not. The problem with such guidelines is that it is important that GPs should be actively involved in the process if it is to have a useful end result. This inevitably requires meetings and the progress may be slow as each specialty must be reviewed individually and only at a rate that the group can accommodate. Another possibility is to formalize arrangements for referral between GPs in a practice or even within a locality where particular GPs may have a particular interest in a certain specialty and where it might be practical for them to take referrals (under contract) from other GPs in the locality.

The Exeter Trust Director (*see* Box 7.4) may seem doubtful as to whether referrals can be controlled in this way but there is every reason to believe that they can in a similar way to prescribing patterns. In North

West Bristol, for instance, a similar process has led to a 20% reduction in spinal X-rays. The same group has persuaded the health authority to identify a number of orthopaedic outpatient appointments for the LCG. This then gives the group the option of either keeping to this specified number, which means that patients do not have to wait, or going over this limit and thus increasing patient waiting times.

Reduced inpatient hospital care

Increasing day case surgery and earlier hospital discharges both reduce the overall hospital bill. Similarly, early discharge to a community hospital, nursing home or hospital at home service will reduce the length of stay in the district general hospital. In these ways a greater number of beds are made available for emergency admissions. Meanwhile, emergency medical units are working with LCGs to see how they can reduce the number of emergency inpatient hospital admissions and various solutions are emerging such as fast track clinics and same day assessments by consultant staff. All these options need to be negotiated between managers, consultants and GPs with the realization that although reducing hospital costs may reduce overall costs there is a need to finance the alternatives. For instance, if a commissioning group and a health authority decide to reduce inpatient facilities for the acute mentally ill they may need to institute an effective and better resourced 24-hour service provided by community psychiatric nurses.

Better communication

Better communication between GPs and consultants may obviate unnecessary referrals and admissions. An outpatient appointment may be prevented by direct communication with the consultant by telephone or letter or cross-referral to another GP in the practice. An emergency admission may be prevented by direct communication with support from a senior hospital doctor, which may be a better option than the traditional one of admitting a patient under the most junior member of the medical staff.

Looking for cheaper options

At an advanced level of sophistication and trust, consultants and GPs may be able to agree to change practice to a cheaper option. This will usually involve the transfer of work from secondary to primary care. For instance, if practice nurses can be directly trained by a trust to deal with eye casualties or do pre-operative checks for eye operations then this saves the work of a specialist service and is likely to be a cheaper option and more convenient for the patient as it is offered locally. The *quid pro quo* is that the trust, the health authority and the LCG will need to agree to the transfer of some money from the specialist contract into primary care with the recognition by all concerned that the overall pot of money can then go further. Integrated nursing schemes in the community have demonstrated the potential to both save money and improve services in this way.

These examples show how purchaser/provider meetings involving the health authority, LCG, trust and consultants can progress towards co-operative problem solving. For instance, specifying a maximum number of cancelled outpatient clinics may be a straightforward purchasing decision but extending the issue to look at how GPs and consultants can both liaise in preventing cancelled appointments and cancelled clinics becomes more of a joint task. Once GPs and consultants get together it seems that just about anything can happen. One of the strengths of locality commissioning is that it has brought them together to co-operate rather than separating them as protagonists in the market place. This is the view expressed by the consultant ophthalmologist in Box 7.5.

Developing a flexible system of purchasing so that money can be moved from primary to secondary care and between different categories of secondary care

The pattern of demand for secondary care is altering (e.g. a greater need for coronary angiograms and by-pass operations) and there is an increasing realization that primary care has the potential to do some of the work presently done in the secondary sector. One of the unfulfilled hopes of fundholding was that it might provide a mechanism for transferring work from secondary to primary care. Nevertheless, there does need to be a mechanism for the 'virement' of resources between different specialties and between the primary and secondary care sectors. The present system makes this very difficult. If a health authority downsizes its contract for a specialty then this may result in redundancy, closure of the specialty and even threaten the integrity of the whole trust itself. Alternatively, the trust with its fixed costs simply compensates when less is being purchased from it by increasing the price of the remainder that is being purchased. Some LCGs have been instrumental in changing large contracts (e.g. the South Tyne Commissioning Group changed its drugs and alcohol contract from one provider to another in 1997) but this is a rarity. If the aim of locality commissioning is to improve local services provided by local trusts then closing down a trust or severely threatening a unit may seem like shooting

Box 7.5: A consultant's view of purchasing with an LCG

(Mr John Jacob, Consultant Ophthalmologist, Royal Devon & Exeter Healthcare NHS Trust)

Consultants generally prefer to concentrate on clinical matters and dislike a lot of interference from management on commissioning or contracting issues which have become a prominent factor in recent health reforms.

Our experience of dealing with general practitioner/LCGs within the general framework of the NHS has led to an improvement in our feelings towards such issues. Locality commissioning means dealing with a body representing a large number of patients and GPs which makes more sense than dealing with individual GPs as often happens with GP fundholders. The consultants and GP commissioning groups can then have a significant influence on the overall purchasing by the health authority resulting in general benefit to patient care.

Direct contact between leaders of the GP commissioning group and the consultants means more direct clinician to clinician discussion which has led to a greater understanding of each other's problems. The consultants have been able to appreciate the concerns of the GP on specific and general aspects of care and service delivery. Such problems can then be examined by the consultant and responded to in a less bureaucratic and non-threatening atmosphere. Simple concerns, such as the length of time it takes for a letter to return to GPs, can be discussed openly and appropriate action taken immediately to try and satisfy all demands.

Better understanding between primary and secondary health care groups resulting from such a meeting has led to an easier exchange of ideas. In the field of ophthalmology we have been able to develop practice nurse to nurse practitioner exchanges between general practice and the ophthalmology unit in order to try and prevent unnecessary casualty referrals. This will lead to further development of a shared care basis for the management of some patients and an ability to educate patients about eye problems and for them to feel confident about approaching their general practice rather than immediately seeking secondary referral.

continued opposite

Box 7.5: *continued*

All of these factors make the GP commissioning group a much easier group to deal with than others and will lead to an overall better understanding between consultants and GPs and primary and secondary health care management. Consultants will be much more likely to respond to ideas and plans proposed by a respected and well balanced group such as an LCG.

itself in the foot. Some total purchasing projects may not have such qualms and say that inefficient companies are cutting down and closing every day, so why not trusts within the NHS? In a way this is their only option as total purchasing projects are (in theory at least) confined only to purchasing as a mechanism for change. LCGs have at least two options for viring resources between one category of care and another.

Fixing health authority budgets at locality level

If a locality has an identified budget and if there is sufficiently good information to determine what is being purchased with this budget then it becomes possible for the LCG to be instrumental in reducing or cost-limiting expenditure in one area (e.g. extra contractual referrals, asymptomatic varicose veins or school nursing) and use any money saved for another service. In this way, for instance, money for minor surgery that can be done in general practice can be vired from the secondary sector for it to be done there. For reasons discussed, the level of virement is likely to be relatively small but it does not require the LCG to take on any responsibility for the locally identified budget itself. It could help, for instance, a cash pressed locality to provide a locality back pain clinic staffed by a local GP. In future, if localities either choose to or are impelled to take on prescribing budgets then this could provide other possibilities for virement.

Merging purchasing and planning role

If there is a need to rationalize services (e.g. merge a service in two trusts into one provided from one trust) then co-operative planning will achieve this purpose in a far better way than the cut and thrust of purchasing alone.

By meeting with all the stakeholders, a health authority and its locality GPs can tell trust representatives what they are going to be willing to purchase in the future and thereby give a trust time to plan for change in an organized manner. With major changes this may involve several LCGs and several trusts meeting in this way to try and rationalize future services (*see* Chapter 6). By this means LCGs can have a fundamental say in the development of individual services such as day case surgery and the treatment of the acute mentally ill through to the development and provision of whole hospitals.

Purchasing dilemmas

In future LCGs will be faced with questions which they will need to decide upon and answer.

Can LCGs purchase effectively without a budget?

This question has perhaps been already answered in this chapter. Trust behaviour and service specifications can all be effectively altered without a budget. Indeed none of the work described so far in this chapter has required any budgetary interest on the part of the LCG. Nevertheless, some health authorities are proposing identified locality budgets and some LCGs are welcoming them because it provides them with a potentially tighter hold on what is going on within the locality and a better idea of where changes can be effected. They might also ease the process of virement though it has to be said that their worth is unproven. Dr Ashok Vora expresses a wish for financial involvement in saying 'We have achieved a certain degree of beneficial change simply by dialogue and persuasion. To go further we feel we must be in a position to quantify the financial impact of discussions with trusts and, if need be, to move monies in pursuit of our commissioning intentions. Otherwise our ability to bring about real change is limited'.

If there is an identified locality budget, an LCG can still decide how it is going to relate to it. In some circumstances, an LCG may state categorically that such a locality budget is not its responsibility but that of the health authority, which has delegated it to its locality management team. Alternatively, the LCG may wish to identify some areas of activity for which it is happy to accept such joint budgetary responsibility. Finally, an LCG might wish to take on much fuller joint budgetary responsibility and this would entail a fuller integration of the LCG and its locality management team (*see* Chapter 10).

The issue of who holds the budget is a largely sterile one and there is nothing implicitly good about a commissioning group taking on joint responsibility for a budget if the devolved officers of the health authority are able to do it adequately. What happens in any individual case is more likely to depend on the relationship of trust between the group and the management team and the purchasing and financial proficiency of the management team and the health authority itself rather than more fundamental issues of principle. If a group wishes for greater budgetary autonomy then it must accept more accountability and responsibility in return. Each locality group will need to decide where it stands on these issues but, as already emphasized, it would be inappropriate to force any locality group to accept a budget of any sort if it is either unable or unwilling to do so – premature moves of this sort would be more likely to disrupt and possibly destroy an LCG altogether.

Is the GP's role as GP advocate in conflict with that of taking joint purchasing responsibility with the local health authority?

This is possibly a case of render unto Caesar what is Caesar's. In the surgery the GP is the patient's advocate. Outside the surgery, in his or her role as a co-operative strategic purchaser, he or she is the advocate for the whole of the local population. This patient advocacy role may be challenged further when there is an identified budget for the locality particularly if the LCG is happy to take co-operative responsibility for such a budget. Nevertheless, the GP can wear two hats provided that he or she does not wear two hats at the same time. It is interesting that in some LCGs, where a strong group consensus has been established, the GPs are recognizing a need for an arbitration process to defend the individual GP's right to stand up for an individual patient when a patient's needs or demands are not apparently being met by the specifications agreed by the group in general.

Purchasing primary care and GP services

A mechanism that was originally devised for purchasing secondary care can, in theory, be adapted to the purchasing of primary care as well. There is a problem here, however, because GPs are not only the main providers of primary care but also independent contractors to the NHS. The National Association of Commissioning GPs has, therefore, quite properly stated that LCGs should not be involved in purchasing primary care for their own community. Thus LCGs should stick to commissioning primary care while health authorities retain all responsibility for purchasing primary care. This fine line may be challenged by two possible scenarios.

1 If general practice was de-regulated, LCGs might want to take on an advisory purchasing role in order to safeguard the quality of services, which had previously been provided by member practices. If they took on such a role they would need to demonstrate that they were acting in the interests of patients in the locality rather than in the interests of the GPs themselves.
2 The merger of FHSAs with health authorities and the creation of locality management teams means that such teams are inevitably responsible for both primary and secondary care in the locality. As LCGs begin to work closer with these locality management teams they may be tempted to become involved in some primary care purchasing decisions. These may include, for instance, decisions to reimburse GPs for acute nursing home admissions, anticoagulation clinics or increased minor surgery. An awareness of the potential conflict of roles is all that may be necessary.

Joint purchasing

It does not make sense to plan health services in isolation from everything else and increasingly health authorities and LCGs are looking at joint planning strategies with other agencies when drawing up their locality health strategies. Similarly, purchasing in isolation leads to lines of demarcation and patients will inevitably fall between the crevices of separately purchased services. To prevent this there is a need for joint purchasing of certain services and an LCG provides a good local basis for such combined activity especially, for instance, with social services.

Clear agreements between the locality management team, LCG and social services have reduced (if not totally prevented) the collusion of anonymity, which has typified the care of patients who come under both banners. The cultures of health service and social service purchasing have gradually grown apart and a realignment is long overdue.

It is frequently said that LCGs are just talking shops with no teeth. A co-operative involvement in purchasing with the DHA allows the LCG to have as many potential teeth as it needs. Its bite, however, is derived from its role as planner. In general it will achieve much more by being a placid herbivore and need only behave like a Tyrannosaurus Rex when it meets the same.

8 Evidence, audit and information technology

Locality commissioning groups (LCGs) need proper access to evidence if they are to make informed commissioning decisions. Similarly, individual GPs, practices and the locality as a whole will need good access to evidence when making individual and collective clinical decisions. That being said, a commitment to using best evidence should not exclude the possibility of using treatments that are not conclusively proven one way or the other nor should it become a tyranny to challenge the primacy of making the right clinical decision for each individual patient.

Audit, on the other hand, provides a means whereby an LCG can assess whether its involvement in the commissioning process has produced the desired effect. Groups can assess their effectiveness by commissioning group audits or by choosing interested practices to do them. At practice level it is equally necessary for practices to assess whether they are achieving the results that they are aiming for. As practices within a locality start moving closer together a third form of audit is beginning to emerge, which looks at locality performance not purely in its commissioning role but also in its collective provider role. An example might be a locality audit on the secondary prevention of coronary events. Consequently, it is important that evidence and audit should be available at all three levels – the practice, the collective provider unit of practices within a locality and finally the commissioning group itself.

Audit is the fourth and final stage of the commissioning process (*see* Chapter 1). It is also the first stage of the next commissioning cycle where the results of audit, needs assessment (*see* Chapter 5) and evidence will all provide information towards the next stage of planning and purchasing. The collection, processing and provision of all this information require adequate information technology, which commissioning groups will also need to access in the future.

This chapter reviews the use of evidence and audit from the perspective of a primary care audit group manager and the need for information technology as perceived by a fundholding GP, who also belongs to an LCG.

Evidence – taking action to enhance effective health care

Liz Cosford and Donald McLintock

Promoting clinical effectiveness within the health service culture is no easy task. Many clinicians will argue that the care they provide has been and always will be based on evidence whether that be from the literature in the form of books and journals or from past experience and knowledge. All these forms of gathering evidence are as important as each other but used together can only enhance an effective health care service. The contentious issues within primary care and ones which are not easily resolved overnight are how to access the evidence – especially when you are a busy GP based within a consulting room – when should you consider changing practice as a result of evidence being presented and how do you know that once you think you have implemented the evidence it is actually being sustained? These are all key questions for general practice in the 1990s, but the same issues also apply within the locality commissioning framework and the opportunities that these groups have in improving the services that are being commissioned locally.

The main issues to consider when supporting an evidence-based framework are considered in Figure 8.1.

Finding the evidence

Where do you find the evidence? What are the main resources available to practices and commissioning groups to find the evidence? A possible list includes:

- postgraduate medical library
- general practice library

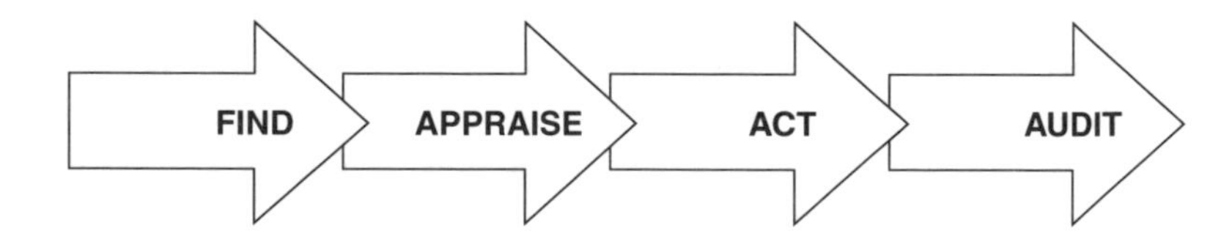

Figure 8.1: Stages in creating an evidence-based framework.

- books
- journals
- media
- bibliographic databases such as Medline, Cinhal, Cochrane
- Cochrane collaboration.

National sources include the NHS centre for reviews and dissemination which develops systematic reviews and the Royal Colleges. This may all take time, which is something that a busy GP has very little of. In order to save time, there are some useful journals that have been developed nationally such as:

- *Bandolier*
- *Effective Healthcare*
- *Effectiveness Matters.*

All these journals have information regarding the latest evidence and collate this in order for practitioners to consider how they might change their own practice.

If a practice has a good library then accessing the evidence becomes easier and other options are to subscribe to Medline and to gain access to computer information, which can put practices in contact with the NHS wideweb and bring evidence to the desk top. The development of computer-based access within a practice will be a key to accessing evidence in the future.

Within LCGs, the locality medical directors and health authority managers have access to other library services such as a library based within the health authority. It is essential that a system is in place within the health authority so that the locality groups have access and are aware of all new clinical effectiveness articles such as the *Effective Health Care* bulletins which are widely circulated. These can help inform future work, such as developing a locality-based clinical audit project and the same applies for new research articles that are published.

Appraising or evaluating the evidence

Every week many research articles are published in journals. The skill of appraising a research paper is very important and essential when considering whether to change practice or not. It would be wrong to assume that any paper published in a journal has already been appraised by the review panel. This is often not the case although a review panel is, of course, asked to review the paper before publication. Critical appraisal of evidence requires two steps:

1 deciding whether it is valid

2 deciding whether it is important.

Nationally, a model has been developed, which is called Critical Appraisal Skills for Purchasers (CASP). The aim is to help guide clinicians through a research paper to assess both of these criteria. In the North & East Devon District the primary care audit group and the research and development unit have locally adapted the model and developed training sessions called 'Evidence Made Easy' for general practices. The model consists of reading a research paper and then answering ten questions about it which will guide clinicians to make an informed assessment of the paper. The training sessions are focused at the multi-professional team not just doctors and help engage every member to consider the evidence put before them. Engaging clinicians in this type of event has been difficult and it is through the commitment of the LCGs that this type of approach has been successful. It is very important to select papers that are relevant to the local community and the LCGs can help to advise. It is just as important that LCGs themselves undergo this type of training to help inform future commissioning decisions.

Acting on the evidence

It has been shown that within the health care setting it can take years to implement and change practice. In 1969, for example, a huge body of evidence based on large randomized controlled trials established that long-term medium dose aspirin therapy (75–325 mg/day) protects against myocardial infarction, stroke or vascular death in those patients at high risk of vascular disease. Nevertheless, it took up to 20 years for this to be implemented and for it to be recommended in textbooks for clinicians.

There is evidence that when new evidence and guidelines are published and disseminated through traditional routes it makes very little difference to the bulk of medical practice. It seems to affect only those innovators who actively seek out such new evidence. Several techniques, however, can be used to change clinical behaviour and listed below are some of the types of activity which could be said to 'engage' the practising doctor or nurse. Engagement does not mean the same as ownership but does imply that the clinician has felt the impact of the new evidence with regard to his or her own practice.

Guidelines

Guidelines have been shown to change behaviour in practising clinicians, but only when the process of constructing the guidelines has involved those who are going to use them in their daily work, e.g. a primary health care team or community hospital. Though local guidelines tend to be less scientifically valid than those which are researched and presented by national groups representing all interested parties, they are more likely to be taken up and used by those involved and consequently change behaviour.

Consultation

It is important that any new guidelines being disseminated from expert bodies is presented to local practitioners in order for them to review its local application and make appropriate amendments. A half or full day seminar with participation of many local clinicians has been shown to be effective in increasing use of guidelines. It helps those who are unable to attend or who are not vocal to air their thoughts in writing before or during the meeting. This process would fit well into locality commissioning.

Practice visits

Educational outreach visits have been shown to be effective in changing prescribing behaviour both to start new drugs and stop ineffective ones. Pharmaceutical houses spend vast amounts of money doing this and have found it a highly effective method of changing prescribing behaviour. Visits to practices by local community pharmacists sponsored by health authorities, using similar techniques to pharmaceutical reps, can make positive and unbiased changes to prescribing behaviour.

Audit

Single audits (reviews) have been shown to be poor at changing behaviour but the prospect of joining an audit spiral where behaviour will be re-measured does seem to be effective (the Hawthorne Effect). Passive feedback of audit, e.g. by posting results, has little effect on the majority of practitioners. When the results are discussed either at a locality meeting (as described above) or during a visit by a respected peer or by the practice team it is likely that changes in clinical behaviour will be significant. It is important that practice managers or administrative staff are involved in any discussions which might involve changes in their work.

Specific trigger protocols

A very effective way of changing behaviour is to build the evidence into a computer protocol which appears automatically under certain trigger circumstances. Computer protocols and templates are used in general practice, especially by practice nurses. There is little published work in this field as far as general practice is concerned though it is being investigated by the *Prodigy* project. Evidence from hospital practice and the business community suggests that it ought to be effective and keeping the information in a drawer or a background computer file results in little change. Locality commissioning could develop these information technology resources to introduce new activity or maintain appropriate standards in current practice.

Financial inducements

Drug companies found this so effective that the ABPI had to be persuaded to ban this method of behaviour modification. However, health authorities enhance certain portions of practice budgets to maintain the Department of Health targets for vaccination and cervical cytology. An LCG could theoretically agree that a specific activity would be beneficial to its population and then use either a voluntary 'carrot' or a mandatory 'stick' in order to achieve a communally agreed benefit. Such action might encourage changes in care in practices that were resistant to or had difficulty in attending academic sessions.

In these ways locality commissioning offers a greater potential than ever before for GPs in a locality to access, use and successfully implement new evidence that collectively they feel to be appropriate.

Audit

Liz Cosford

Clinical audit

In 1989, the White Paper *Working for Patients* saw medical audit formally introduced into the health service. Audit seeks to improve the quality and outcome of patient care through structured peer review. It requires clinicians to examine their practices and results against agreed standards and to modify their practice where indicated. In 1993 the focus shifted to clinical audit, which meant that this was seen as an important function for all health care professionals and not just medics. This has been sustained within the health service.

Clinical audit offers a practical way for local clinicians to review their own practice and thereby improve the care given to patients. In this way cost-effective audit can be developed which can lead to demonstrable benefits for the NHS.

In general practice there are two main types of audit. The first is a conventional audit project which is designed in detail to look at a certain area of care, and the second is a process called 'significant event audit'. This chapter focuses on conventional audit. Clinical audit is important in improving the locality purchasing arrangements, e.g. waiting times, discharge summaries or clinical outcomes (based on practice-based audits). It also has a role within the practice to help us answer the question 'Are we doing what we should be doing?' This is particularly important in chronic diseases, when there is strong evidence about what we should be doing. A number of PCAGs offer 'off the shelf' or district-wide audits, which allow practices to participate and then check their performance against their peers and provide a locality or district average. These centrally developed audits are usually evidence-based and extensively piloted. They save practices considerable time in the planning stage as well as providing an audit of known quality.

Developing a conventional audit

The benefits of undertaking a conventional audit are that it will help members of a practice to establish how good their care is against set standards and identify if they are not meeting those standards. It should also tell them whether there are basic factors that need rectifying in order for them to improve. For example, if the practice nurse and receptionists identify that there are an increased number of calls from patients who wish to receive their cervical smear results from the practice an audit can be undertaken to find out why this is happening. The audit could identify that the patients are not being informed of how they will receive their results or that they do not understand the procedure and are, therefore, ringing the receptionist for details which is causing extra, potentially unnecessary work for the receptionist and the practice nurse.

Figure 8.2 demonstrates the model for developing a simple practice-based audit. The hardest part of the cycle is changing practice. In order to help this process it is essential that everyone involved in the care of the patient for a particular project is involved at the beginning. If everyone understands why a project is being developed then they are more likely to understand why it is important for them to improve their practice as much as it is for everyone else in the team and thus overall care can be improved. It is also essential, if any changes have been made, that the project is

Establish problem

Review standards

Set standards

Evaluate change

Measure practice

Compare against standards

Implement change

Identify opportunity for improvement

Suggest change

Figure 8.2: The audit cycle (*BMJ*, 1990).

re-audited. If this is not done then the changes that have been implemented may actually cause the standard of care to deteriorate rather than improve.

A step-by-step guide for a conventional audit is shown in Box 8.1.

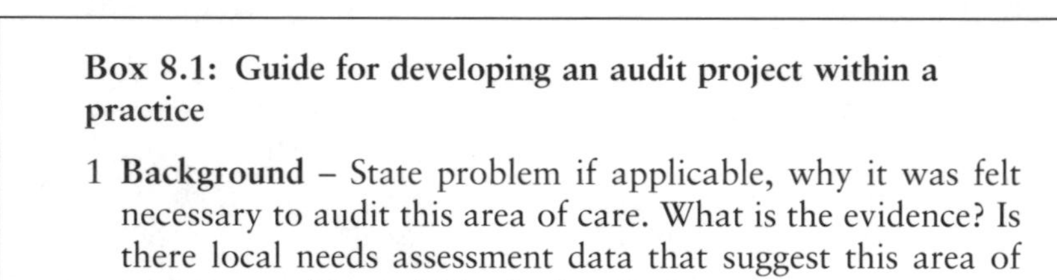

Box 8.1: Guide for developing an audit project within a practice

1 **Background** – State problem if applicable, why it was felt necessary to audit this area of care. What is the evidence? Is there local needs assessment data that suggest this area of care is a problem within the locality?
2 **Aim of project** – What do you want to achieve from the audit?
3 **Standards** – Specify standards to be measured which should be evidence-based wherever possible.
4 **Methods** – Consider how the information is to be collected (retrospectively, prospectively).
5 **Sample size** – State how you are going to select your sample.
6 **Timescale** – State when you want to begin/end/re-audit.
7 **Professional groups who should participate in audit including patients** – Ensure all professionals involved in providing care to the patient are involved. Consider whether it is appropriate to involve a patient.

Commissioning groups can use the same model when undertaking or commissioning audit whether they are contract or service audits or locality-based clinical audits. For example, to establish if a provider unit is maintaining care within their contract limits, such as waiting times, it is necessary to assess whether all patients referred to that unit are being seen within the set standard. A simple audit project can then be developed by the LCG to establish (a) how far the provider unit is from meeting its contract and (b) if the contract is not being met, why not? Ownership of the auditing process entails that LCGs feel committed to solutions that are designed to rectify problems that emerge from this process.

Using local needs data to inform locality-based audit projects

Local needs data are now essential in informing the delivery of health care for the future. The information regarding the local needs data can be obtained from public health departments (*see* Chapter 5) but is also obtainable from the local health strategies (*see* Chapter 6). From this information, clinical audit projects can be identified by the LCGs and conventional projects developed. For example, the local needs data may identify that there is a high level of termination of pregnancies in a rural locality. By commissioning a conventional audit the reasons may identify that access to the family planning service is poor, that patients do not understand the concept of emergency contraception and that particularly in those under 16 years, patients do not go to their GP for advice. This information can be fed into the locality health strategies and can also help inform future purchasing and planning decisions, which may affect the locality. A similar project can be developed if the local needs data identify a high mortality rate in certain disease areas, for example skin cancer, or identify high hospitalization rates, for example asthma where primary care intervention may be appropriate and effective.

The role of the primary care audit group in locality commissioning

Each primary care audit group will work in a geographical area including a number of localities. Increasingly PCAGs see the advantages of working closely, if not actually within, health authorities. This is a far cry from the early days when separation was the order of the day and MAAGs were debating issues around separation from FHSAs, confidentiality and whether the medical adviser or director of public health should be part of the group.

Increasingly, the priorities of the health authority are synonymous with those of primary care and the LCGs. The close relationship between health authorities and PCAGs can be of even more benefit if translated to LCGs. This synergism has three main functions.

1. To align agendas (priority setting) building on local needs assessment.
2. To address the health needs of local communities as well as those of individuals.
3. To develop effectiveness within health care (clinical effectiveness).

Priority setting

Health authorities and LCGs derive their agenda from a multitude of sources (Box 8.2) and through a process of prioritization an achievable workload is generated. To ensure maximum impact, especially in primary care, it is essential that PCAGs are linked into the locality process.

Box 8.2: Agenda setting

National	Health of the Nation Mental health Cancers	Evidence-based practice – Effectiveness bulletins – Evidence-based medicine
District	Commissioning process Contracting Audit process Value for money	
Local communities	Needs assessment Practice problems Local problems Community health councils	

Structures

Each LCG should have at least one representative on their PCAG, either a GP, practice manager, practice nurse or a combination. This ensures effective communication between health professionals at district and locality level and also, importantly, with individual practices. There is a need for a parallel system of management links at these high levels again involving the PCAG. The managers within the locality framework need an effective system of communication with the practice manager on the PCAG, and also individual practice managers. They are key people who act as effective links between localities and all the individual practice team members. These two important elements of communication are not mutually exclusive, but general practices have different styles, and more than one system is required to cope with this diversity. Primary care audit groups can play a pivotal role in delivering high-quality/cost-effective health care within a district partly because they have the experience of collaborating with other agencies and of developing large district-wide audit projects.

Developing projects

Primary care audit groups should also be working with LCGs to identify priority areas for audit in the future which may impact on primary care, secondary care, community care and other agencies. Audit projects for LCGs will develop from the following sources:

- new or old research – developing an evidence-based audit project
- local needs data of the locality which can identify unusual trends in both morbidity and mortality data.

Where projects have been identified then the primary care audit group can take a leading role in identifying the key stakeholders and engaging them in the project. The overall project management can be delegated to the primary care audit group who has the experience of setting up large multi-professional, cross-boundary, district-wide projects. Sometimes the project may be cross-boundary and in these circumstances an interface project may be appropriate.

Interface audit projects

Interface audit projects have been recently developed in North & East Devon. Topics have been identified from Health of the Nation targets and/or an evidence base. The primary care audit group identified all the relevant clinicians who should be involved in the different health care agencies and takes on the responsibility of setting up and overseeing the maintenance of the project. Patients are also involved wherever appropriate. The steering group is set up to design, implement and make recommendations for change. In order to get ownership from all sectors of health care within the district it is essential to involve key clinicians who will not only help inform the steering group but will also communicate the aims of the project to their colleagues in their organization/primary care. An example of an interface audit project is shown in Box 8.3.

Box 8.3: An interface audit of pain-to-needle time

The aim of this project was to establish the timeliness of current practice in the thrombolytic treatment of myocardial infarction (MI) in the North & East Devon District. It also intended to identify any areas of preventable delays where practice could be improved.

A multi-professional steering group was set up with a remit to design and develop the project. Membership of the group consisted of the following professionals from across the district:

- consultant cardiologists
- general practitioners
- West Country ambulance service
- sister from coronary care unit
- clinical audit staff
- primary care audit group.

Recommendations

1 It is inappropriate for suspected MIs to be admitted to community hospitals.
2 Need to educate the public with regard to the appropriate conduct in the event of acute chest pain.
3 Education of junior doctors regarding local guidelines should take place during induction.
4 All GPs should be aware of the clinical guidelines to admit a patient immediately if chest pain continues for longer than 20 minutes.

Actions

1 Education of junior doctors incorporated into regular induction programme.
2 Working with clinical tutors, guidelines have been developed and awareness has been heightened through postgraduate school newsletter and study days.
3 Working with the Health of the Nation team, issues to address public awareness are being discussed. Media is to be involved.

The role of the PCAG in contract and service audit

This role is debatable and the decision to involve the primary care audit group in this subject is very much a local decision. The majority of PCAGs do not get involved in this type of audit at the present time as their expertise may be best spent in developing clinical audit projects across a district. At present such audits tend to be done on an 'ad hoc' basis either by the group itself or one or two individual practices. Frequently, the group depends upon audits done by the health authority or its relevant locality management team and internal audits done by the trusts themselves.

Research

For those undertaking research, a locality structure provides an excellent opportunity to recruit active practices in localities and controls. Developing and assessing a new intervention/service in one locality can be swiftly implemented in other localities if it is proved to be effective.

The Department of Health in its document *Promoting Clinical Effectiveness* provides the triangular model of *Inform*, *Monitor*, *Change*. This simple framework is particularly useful at locality level. Localities are small enough to offer an environment of friendship, mutual trust, commitment and the peer support of local practices. They are also large enough to provide the economy of scale that allows effective education, peer audit and research to take place. The challenge for the future will be for centralized audit, education and research centres to adapt to the locality model and recognize these possibilities of interacting with and reaching every GP.

Information technology and locality commissioning

Mark Couldrick

Information is power. Planning requires information. These rather glib statements contain important messages. If locality commissioning is to develop from a forum for advising health authorities into an informed and authoritative structure for guiding the provision of both secondary and community care then it must do so supported by robust data.

Information technology (IT) and fundholding have largely revolved around the need to monitor transactions at practice level to ensure that they are or are not chargeable to the fund. Locality commissioning of all services abolishes the need for this labour and time intensive task but should not be seen as a cheap option. Health authority and provider units now have fairly good data on secondary care activity. This can be helpful in guiding commissioning but inevitably only reflects a small fraction of the actual morbidity in the community. The grouping together of practices in a locality is an opportunity to use data on primary care morbidity for the first time to inform planning and purchasing decisions. Successful locality commissioning requires a detailed understanding of local health needs and the priorities of local populations, and also a knowledge of how to meet these needs and priorities. Various projects around the country are starting to collect morbidity data to this end.[1] The data are starting to be used to help commission services on the basis of local need.[2]

There are practical difficulties due to the great variety of GP systems. Health authorities that have taken a co-ordinating role in primary care computing are starting to reap the benefit. Over the next few years, however, few bodies involved in planning and commissioning care (whether at health authority or locality level) will be able to manage without data collected in this way. The investment in IT offered to fundholders allowed the development of clinical systems in parallel with fund management systems. Conversely practices not involved in fundholding have often suffered from serious lack of IT investment. Among many GPs there has been a reluctance to embrace GP computing and it has frequently been seen as a very limited tool for repeat prescribing and a few disease registers. Indeed, the value of data collected by the recording of all primary care patients in a retrievable form is just starting to be recognized and used.

Health authorities and trusts should provide data on activity from secondary care preferably processed in a way to make it digestible and easily used. Practices should concentrate on the development of their own IT strategies for the use of computing to facilitate information gathering in primary care and must be supported by appropriate investment from the bodies which will start to use this data. This will require localities to survey the provision of IT within their practices and develop a clear plan to support and facilitate practice IT with both money and expertise.

It is also important to recognize the great power of computing for audit in locality commissioning. It is required not only to assess standards in secondary care but also to audit standards in primary care itself. General practitioners need to become used to using comparative data on activities such as prescribing rates, referral rates, imaging and laboratory medicine usage at practice and doctor level. They also need to recognize that the information needs to be open for examination by commissioning groups in order to understand local patterns of care, and this might affect the need for future service provision. Non-computer literate practices will have to rely on this data being accurate.

The great challenge of locality commissioning is to take forward the widespread implementation of evidence-based primary care practice and the commissioning of care according to local needs assessment. This can only be achieved if GPs are empowered with the information that they require to fulfil their role as providers and increasingly as commissioners of care.

References

1 NHSE Information Management Group (1996) *Collection of Health Data from General Practice (CHDGP) project*. NHSE, Leeds.
2 Pearson N, O'Brien J, Thomas H, Ewings P, Gallier L, Bussey A (1996) Collecting morbidity data in general practice: the Somerset morbidity project. *BMJ* **312**: 1517–20.

Further reading

Meads G (1996) *A Primary Care-Led NHS – Putting it into Practice*. Churchill Livingstone, Edinburgh.
NHS Executive (1996) *Primary Care: The Future*. NHSE, Leeds.
NHS Executive (1996) *Clinical Guidelines. Using clinical guidelines to improve patient care within the NHS*. NHSE, Leeds.
NHS Executive (1996) *Promoting Clinical Effectiveness. A framework for action in and through the NHS*. NHSE, Leeds.
NHS Executive (1996) *Clinical Audit in the NHS, Using Clinical Audit in the NHS: a position statement*. NHSE, Leeds.
NHS Centre for Reviews and Dissemination (1997) *Effective Healthcare, Preventing and Reducing the Adverse Effects of Unintended Teenage Pregnancies*. University of York, York.
NHS Care for Reviews and Dissemination (1995) *Effectiveness Matters, Aspirin and Myocardial Infarction*. University of York, York.
Sackett DL, Scott Richardson W, Rosenberg W, Haynes RB (1997) *Evidence-based Medicine. How to Practice and Teach EBM*. Churchill Livingstone, Edinburgh.

9 Accountability

In a consumer conscious age that is tired of sleeze overtones in public life, commissioning groups will be expected to be more open and involve a wider group of people than ever before. This expectation may be partly a result of the lack of accountability during the early years of fundholding – an accountability framework which required fundholders to make explicit their actions in a number of ways was not published until several years after fundholding had already been established. A few of these early fundholders were seen as go-getters for personal gain and though they may have reinforced an image that fitted the Tory ethos of self-determination, this philosophy sat uncomfortably with public service values. Contrary political dogma that supports the underdog through benevolent public service will see a theme of greater democracy in decision-making and an expectation of fairness in service delivery. But the inheritance of a market-driven system linked to personal gain will not be lightly thrown off. A wholesale return to a distant memory of vocational practitioners doing their best for the poor and sick may never be realized.

To work, GP commissioning will need to provide rewards for those who will carry it out, which will include both supporting the work financially and possibly offering extra for the increased local services and local facilities that are brought about in this way. It is a tribute to the success of GP co-ops that sufficient resources were made available to support their establishment but not in such great quantities as to be accused of greed nor too little to undervalue it. Steering that course for GP commissioning will be vital to meet the expectations of the workforce and for it to be accepted as reasonable by public critics. GP commissioning is seen as a more politically defensible system because it can distinguish between the commissioning role, the patient advocacy role and the role of the GP as a businessman/woman within his or her own practice. Patients with expensive needs will not need to fear exclusion from a list as was rumoured to happen with fundholders as their costs will be met from a locality resource where risk is managed beyond an individual practice base.

There are two sides to the accountability coin. One side is to explain why you have done what you have done while the other asks what do you think of what has been done and asks for feedback to inform the next moves. An accountability structure will need to demonstrate both the listening and the decisions taken as a result of it. A strong theme will be to engage local people in understanding and making choices around health care systems. Accountability will also need to take other forms. If some GP commissioning groups wish to share budgetary responsibility then they will need to be accountable to the health authority and under the scrutiny of auditors and financial advisors. They will also need to demonstrate clinical accountability to assure their patients that what they do and what they buy is both safe and effective and driven by patients' needs and their experiences. Finally, it will be important for GP commissioners to be accountable to fellow professionals in the health service and beyond that to a wider network of statutory agencies of which health services are but a part.

Accountability to the local population

Many words, many experiments, much thought and fine rhetoric have been propounded on this topic. The logical starting point is to assume that those at the receiving end of services should be those who can best determine what and how they should be delivered. The 'how' questions are more easily grasped than the 'what' questions. To find out from a patient how the experience of a service felt and how it could be improved is the easy bit. Patient insight into service quality is important feedback. The tricky bit, however, is to decide on the 'what question' with public involvement. Work on how to determine priority services with groups of patients has been slow to develop largely because it is so difficult! If a GP commissioning group had a sudden windfall then probably a few options might be easily suggested and local patients would be able to agree a preferred list of extra primary or secondary services. In reality, however, windfalls are rarely available and this means that decisions about health services are more likely to be about changing present services rather than obtaining more services. Change has to mean doing less of one thing in order to do more of another. Inevitably patient groups will defend their territory. Age, gender and socioeconomic group will all influence personal decision-making. An exercise carried out some time ago asked patients, managers and consultants to rank 20 services in order of priority. Needless to say there was very little common ground. An accountability structure to involve the local population as widely as possible will have to take note of the territories that will be both consciously and unconsciously marked. To develop this there are groups of patients who can be usefully engaged in commenting upon services.

- *The representative.* Most localities will already have a number of 'natural' representatives such as councillors, CHC or JCC members and leaders of patient participation groups, for instance, which an LCG can key into. Alternatively, a locality might set up its own representational group. For instance, some health authorities have locality planning teams designed to involve local patients and these can be adapted for such use. A further alternative might be for practices to each nominate one or two patient representatives (depending upon their size) to produce a patients' forum for co-ordinating with the group. Some have proposed a randomly selected 'jury' system for getting patient views based upon the age/sex registers of each practice. This system may be less useful in getting local people to sign up to commissioning group plans. A patient participation group centred around a particular surgery may have a favourable bias towards it but can be a useful source of informed opinion on surgery performance. Collective feedback from several groups of this sort can provide further useful evidence on locality performance. Developing links with local MPs offer further opportunities to debate local issues. Whatever system is chosen, if it can build upon structures that are already in place then so much the better.
- *The good citizen.* A number of individuals take on citizenship roles in our communities by being councillors, school governors, church wardens, JPs, league of friends, and local leaders of various sorts. They are likely to have the skills in determining the weight of the arguments and measuring the priorities of one thing against another as well as substantive interest in their own local communities.
- *The single interest group.* Many examples exist of single issue groups which are usually organized by highly committed individuals to a single topic area. Such groups can become exceptionally knowledgeable (especially now with widespread Internet access) on their subject area. They can also often raise substantial sums to support their endeavours.
- *The patient experience.* To have been on the receiving end of services will obviously be subjective but it is rare for an individual to have a unique patient experience, and a collective debate on how it felt to receive a particular service can provide useful evidence on its value. Feedback can be undertaken using questionnaires or personal interviews and focus groups have been shown to be particularly useful in raising pertinent issues.

- *The general public.* For most people ill-health is episodic. Few dwell upon the strategic importance of health services outside election times. Engaging people generally in this discussion is likely to prove less worthwhile and less informative than the other groups of patients with whom one might converse. Public opinion formed from media stories will rarely have the opportunity to access the details and meat of the debate. Nevertheless, with specific issues, which need a public mandate it remains important to seek as wide a public debate as possible and not to undervalue the patient education role in the process.

An accountability framework needs to recognize that working with these groups outlined above will require different approaches to engage the right people appropriately. It will also need to explain how decisions are taken by GP commissioning groups and how feedback is received and used.

Techniques involved might include:

- holding commissioning group meetings in public or organizing a public meeting. Special groups can be invited to meetings on particular issues
- making written materials available, e.g. newsletters, annual reports, minutes of meetings and practice plans. These need to be distributed as widely as possible, for instance, to surgeries and public libraries. The local media can frequently be used as they are generally friendly and often hungry for health stories
- managing positive feedback through patient surveys, 'surgeries' and focus groups. Routine meetings with representatives – particularly CHC representatives, JCCs and other voluntary agency fora
- direct representation on a locality group executive or on a sub-locality group (see below)
- appointing a community worker, who is accountable to the local people. He or she would be responsible for keying into the views and experiences of the population and its patients and linking them to the aspirations of local health professionals involved in locality commissioning. This has been a successful model in Newcastle and can ensure the participation of minority groups which may find it difficult to express themselves within the 'medical model'.

These approaches, however worthy, do take time to organize and to get right. The key to successful organization is to be clear from the outset about what outcomes are expected. For some elements of accountability it will be legitimate to say that this is merely a window dressing report of who we are and what we have done. To involve people positively in contributing a view of a service will need more effort than this and getting a structure of local groups of people who meet regularly, receive information and respond to it will take time to work out. Tokenism may be very damaging. To keep people involved they must be allowed to set the agenda. They will also need to see results and be assured that there is proper resourcing for the process with a commitment to equity.

Targeting particular service areas is probably a good way of eliciting a response. Witness what happens when a local hospital is threatened with closure! A GP commissioning group should then set itself some targets. These should be usefully linked to the health strategies where the fine thread of patient need through to a service change can be traced. It could, for example, undertake to consult on two topic areas, write an annual report, publish within the health strategy and hold a public meeting. The acceptance of public service values around openness, responsiveness and sensitivity will underpin this. In Newcastle a commitment to this process of participation, using a community worker, has led to a number of developments. A minor treatment service was established with the closure of a casualty department, access protocols were devised for deaf people using a local trust and a new service was set up to meet the needs of vulnerable families. The GP commissioners in Newcastle have summarized the key ingredients of public consultation as:[1]

- consult as wide a cross-section of the community as possible
- provide appropriate information
- make sure that those participating are adequately supported and resourced
- ensure clear mechanisms for feedback
- honesty and patience, which are paramount.

The health authority has a commitment to hold public consultation about the services that it offers, usually via the purchasing plan. GP commissioning groups will similarly be committed to consultation when they plan a large service change as well as having to give notice to trusts. While there may be rules to be followed, GP commissioning groups need to remind themselves that the reason for becoming commissioners was to be sensitive to their patients' needs, and the very least they can do is listen to the views of those patients through an adequate mechanism for consultation.

Accountability to the health authority and the NHS

In earlier chapters we have described the importance of working closely with the health authority to develop commissioning as a jointly undertaken venture. This needs good faith on both sides, honesty and clarity of purpose. It can also be an area of tension and unease for health authorities if they feel they are giving up their central ground to a maverick band who may take the money and run! What is needed is a framework which accounts closely for the money being spent on behalf of the authority and which is able to meet national and local strategic targets. The difficulty is finding a happy medium that neither reduces the commissioning group's incentive to innovate nor reduces the chief executive of the health authority to waking up in a cold sweat fearful of the implications of sharing or even handing over taxpayers' money to a commissioning group over whom he or she has no control!

So what could this framework of accountability look like? As described earlier there will need to be a form of agreement with the health authority regarding the responsibilities of the group to use any public funds in accordance with the existing financial rules that apply to the NHS as a whole. This sort of 'must do' reminds commissioning groups that whereas GP practices may see themselves as operating as small businesses and can income-generate in some areas, the money coming from the health authority delegating part of their budget is from public funds and must be audited and monitored in accordance with the rules. This agreement should earmark which services are to be either purchased or commissioned on behalf of the authority. Guidelines about monitoring of spending and returning information on this and other contract details will need to be accessible in an agreed format. Agreement about how the resource was allocated and the specification for the services being undertaken with that money will then be clear. This information should also reflect how this service fits the strategic aims either of the NHS or the district with a commitment only to spend money on areas of service to meet patient needs. A reporting schedule will clarify the expectations on each side. For the commissioning group it will be a good discipline to prepare a defence for any proposed service change and to be able to identify the likely numbers, the health gain, the clinical benefits, the cost benefits, etc., before embarking on a purchasing plan.

If a health authority delegates part of its budget to a locality management team working closely with an LCG then it will need to set up a formal sub-committee of the health authority. This should consist of non-executive and executive members together with the lead GPs. This board of management will then be responsible for ensuring appropriate accountability and use of public funds. To help the chief executive sleep more easily he or she might appoint a health authority manager, who can become tied very closely into the commissioning group. His role is not only to ensure that there is a good system of communication around this particular area of work but also to ensure that the work is set in the context of the wider health authority agenda. The management of diversity has been touched upon elsewhere but without wishing to stifle local sensitivity there needs to be some central 'holding of the ring' to keep an acknowledged strategic direction. The strengths of the commissioning group will be in the local implementation of policy and while there may be issues of debate over detail there should be a consensus in the long-term direction, particularly so if the planning cycle has been met and if there has been satisfactory active input from the commissioning group in the first place.

Occasionally there are issues where for one reason or another – usually a knee-jerk political reaction to a notorious media-based case – there is conflict of central NHS priorities with local ones. An example might be the increase in the number of paediatric intensive care beds. GP commissioning groups would be unlikely to want to be involved in purchasing such a rare and expensive resource but may have a view about local cash being directed to an increase in purchasing of this sort. An accountability framework should allow for opportunities for debate between health authorities and commissioning groups on the wider purchasing decisions of the authority especially if resources are to be deducted from the commissioning groups allocation to meet a centrally driven requirement (*see* Chapter 6). Notice periods and a pace of change policy should be negotiated.

Clinical accountability

Locality commissioning decisions must account for local needs (*see* Chapter 5) and be based upon good clinical evidence (*see* Chapter 8). Furthermore, the resulting services should be properly audited (*see* Chapter 8) to ensure that the original criteria have been met. In many ways, this interpretation of accountability, described in the last chapter, is a fairly straightforward process. The problem is more likely to be getting local health workers and patients to sign up to such a system of accountability and to discard historical attitudes and inbuilt prejudices which may hamper such a task. The vociferous GPs and patients in any locality will be clear about they want but the LCG must weigh this against what is clinically necessary and effective.

Involving other professionals

No one doubts that other professionals should be involved, the question is how? As we have already seen (*see* Chapter 4) several groups are beginning

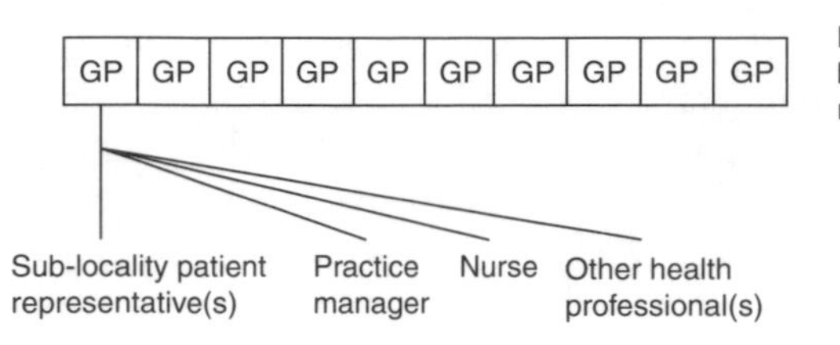

Figure 9.1: A possible scheme for involving local health professionals and patients in commissioning at sub-locality level.

to involve other professionals (e.g. practice managers and nurses) at executive level. Such involvement may come slowly for two reasons. Firstly, GP commissioning groups led by GPs are still in the process of getting on their feet and too many cooks at this stage may spoil the broth. Secondly, if too many people are involved at executive level this leads to a large and increasingly ineffective body for making rapid and decisive plans. Many foresee that GP commissioning/locality commissioning will eventually give way to primary care-led commissioning by a primary care team but it will first need time to show its mettle.

One of the theoretical problems about involving other primary care health workers is that they, like the GPs themselves, are also providers. Furthermore, they are frequently employed by local community trusts and therefore as lead players in the locality they will end up being involved in commissioning decisions with trusts that they actually work for. Besides considerations of size, this may be a further reason why few LCGs at present have other primary health care workers on their boards or executives. Nevertheless, there are other options for involving health workers and the public short of (and possibly as a prelude to) them sitting on the LCG board itself. Figure 9.1 depicts one way in which this work might be done.

In the system illustrated the GP, who is responsible for a sub-locality and who sits on the main board of the LCG, is also responsible for consulting as fully as possible with the public and other health care workers within that sub-locality. One possible way of doing this might be for the GP concerned to have a sub-locality group consisting of one or two patient representatives and possibly a practice manager, nurse representative and one or two representatives of other health care professions. The group could meet from time to time if this seemed appropriate and information and decisions could cascade down from group members to the people that they represent. Feedback could pass upwards along the same route. Such a sub-locality group might even meet with providers within the locality to discuss relevant issues. It would be for the sub-locality GP who sits on the main executive of an LCG to bring items from such meetings to the agenda of the Executive. Where appropriate such sub-locality groups might even develop some budgetary responsibility where it was practical to sub-divide a budget for a particular service within the locality into relevant aliquots for each sub-locality. In this way a sub-locality group could have some real say in how it wishes to use scarce resources.

Whatever the structure and process, the aim must be to inject a sense of common responsibility into all local health professionals and the patient population. By rooting itself ever deeper and ever nearer to each individual patient and each individual health care worker, an LCG can make proper contact with both its patients and its health professionals. If it can do so, then it can be truly said to be representative of the locality and thus worthy of making the important decisions within that locality and at higher levels. These issues will have to be approached sensitively, however, and take into account the views and wishes of the local health professionals themselves, who may often be alienated from the hierarchical structures within their own profession and happier with the more lateral structures, which link individual members of each primary health care team.

For the time being it is important that LCGs simply recognize the wide range of skills that exist within local professional groups and that can usefully contribute to successful commissioning. Analysing needs assessment data, drawing up community profiles, undertaking audits, conducting surveys, arranging work programmes, report writing, running groups and developing business plans are all available resources within primary care at present. The delivery of the preventative health agenda will be largely undertaken by the wider primary care team and their contribution should be recognized and developed well beyond day-to-day tasks.

LCGs have a potential to take the accountability question far further and deeper than ever before. Different arrangements will suit different localities but every group must be prepared to take on the challenge.

Reference

1 Freake D, Crowley P, Steiner M *et al.* (1997) Local heroes. *Health Service Journal* **107** (5561): 28–9.

10 Pilots, prescribing budgets and the pharmaceutical industry

GP commissioning pilots

The setting up of GP commissioning pilots showed an explicit commitment on the part of the government to 'begin a debate on commissioning models for the future'. The 42 pilot schemes are running from April 1998 until April 2000 and will be evaluated by an independent research team. Ironically, they will be financed within fundholding regulations. Each commissioning pilot will have to subscribe to a locality prescribing budget for non-fundholders. Some feel that this is an inevitable part of GP commissioning in the future, while others feel that it adds an unnecessary dimension to the pilot schemes and has little to do with the concept of GP commissioning itself.

Nevertheless, as far as the pilots themselves are concerned they present a first ever opportunity for some GP commissioning groups to access funds for IT and management, to have a fuller say in the development of health authority budgets and to vire resources between different services. Box 10.1 shows the key opportunities as perceived by the Nottingham Total Commissioning Project.

No one can argue with the need to research commissioning groups. Unfortunately, the final results of the pilots will not be clear until well after the turn of the millennium. If the pilots were to be seen as a means of restricting resources to other commissioning groups until the outcome is known then this would be to the detriment of GP commissioning and the NHS. Particularly so as fundholding was introduced without any such stipulations. The need for research should not stifle an equally important and prior need for development. GP commissioning groups throughout the country will need both support and recognition in order to continue such development while the pilots are in progress. Clearly there will need to be guidelines on what constitutes an LCG, its methods of working, the expected outcomes and its accountability structures. The process of

Box 10.1: Key elements of the Nottingham Total Commissioning Pilot

1 Share responsibility between Nottingham Health Authority and core group of elected representative GPs for the deployment of Nottingham Health Authority's budget within an agreed accountability framework. Rationing choices about services will be kept at district rather than practice level.
2 The ability to move money between hospital and prescribing budgets and, where appropriate, into primary care (also known as 'virement').
3 A prescribing budget which is cash-limited at district level with indicative practice amounts. There will be no practice-based prescribing budgets.
4 A locally designed prescribing incentive scheme which is fair and achievable.
5 The development of anonymized feedback about referral patterns, similar to the current PACT arrangement prescribed.
6 Increased funding for GP clinical computer systems.

commissioning will need to be at the heart of any such definition with an entirely voluntary option to become involved in any purchasing or budgetary responsibility. If the rules are sufficiently flexible then other commissioning groups will be able to flourish and develop and thus provide as much useful information on the commissioning debate as the pilots themselves.

Locality prescribing budgets

One condition of joining the pilot projects was the requirement to hold a locality prescribing budget for non-fundholding practices. Each commissioning group had to apply to hold this budget jointly and to achieve a target budget, which was cash limited under the same regulations as fundholding practices. Savings can be vired into local services but only when the whole locality is under budget. Overspends have to be found from health authority cash budgets representing some risk to the health authority as a result.

The need to offer cost-effective and, more importantly, clinically effective outcomes for patients will be ever higher on the agenda. A locality prescribing budget is one device for seeing if costs can be contained in this way and whether a better prescribing practice can be achieved without adversely affecting clinical standards. Thus, it should be possible to test the lever of peer pressure coupled with incentives whereby savings on prescribing can be channelled into more locality services. The need for advice, support and good IT to monitor interventions will all create the opportunity to address the question of how better to use resources and begin the debate on how the wonder drugs of the future can be accommodated. For a locality group this should be a real opportunity to see, for instance, if the prescribing of statins results in the reduction of cardiac events, which ultimately provides the locality groups with savings from needing to purchase less cardiology and cardiac surgery. Simply to constrain a prescribing budget without the prescriber being able to see an outcome runs a danger of encouraging him or her to prescribe more cheaply but possibly less effectively. A marriage between the prescribing outcomes and service usage will need to be developed yet further.

The holding of a locality prescribing budget will challenge the identification of individual GPs within the group and also their ability to manage the process and certainly expose the strengths and weaknesses of the people and the systems engaged in the process. There will be a need to share prescribing information, to develop indicators of good prescribing practice and to get GPs within the group to sign up to these. It seems likely that this aspect of the locality pilots heralds a plan for future cash-limited prescribing budgets in every practice. If so there will be a pressing need for plans to review incentives for dispensing GPs and establish systems of compensation, which stop the absurd system at present whereby the dispensing doctor who prescribes cost effectively runs the danger of reducing his take-home income. Sadly, the setting up of the commissioning pilots did not take these factors into consideration. If GPs lose income in the name of cost-effective prescribing then they will lose an interest both in this and the whole concept of co-operative working with other GPs and the DHA in the process of locality commissioning.

The arrival of expensive drugs in the future will result in some difficult debates for the health service as a whole. Raising prescription charges and removing more drugs from the list that GPs are able to prescribe from will probably be used to reduce demand for products. It is probable that rules for those exempt from paying prescription charges will change as well. These are difficult changes for many GPs to accept along with the prescribing budgets themselves. Nevertheless, to many it has seemed increasingly inevitable that the prescribing blank cheque system that we have at present would at some point become unsustainable. Locality prescribing budgets offer a co-operative solution to the problem and they also offer safety in numbers if and when the ability of clinicians to prescribe effectively begins to come under threat.

Relationship with the pharmaceutical industry

The traditional role of the pharmaceutical industry, which targeted individual clinicians in hospitals and GPs, is developing into one of partnership with health care professionals and policy-makers at a local level. There are, for example, new piecemeal links between pharmaceutical companies and health authorities, primary care audit groups, public health, independent medical advisors and groupings of GPs. An LCG offers an ideal opportunity for streamlining the involvement of pharmaceutical companies within a locality and allows for a co-operative working relationship between all stakeholders who are involved in the planning and provision of health care. Given such a mandate, the partnership between the LCG and the pharmaceutical industry would need clear guidelines.

- *Transparency*. Any agreements between LCGs and private enterprise must be up front, open to view by anyone and with no self-interest on behalf of any individuals or groups within an LCG.
- There should be *no interference with clinical decision-making*, which must be guided solely by an evidence-based process.
- *Agreements must involve all relevant stakeholders*. For instance, if a company is to be involved in a managed care project for strokes then GPs, nurses, allied professionals, consultants and local people will all need to be involved in such a decision.

There are three main areas in which such mutual co-operation is likely to occur.

1 *Sponsorship*. Drug companies are already involved in sponsoring national meetings, the newsletter of the National Association of Commissioning GPs and in providing educational grants for reports and meetings of local groups. It is likely that more sponsorship money will become available for local groups in the future possibly including audit and research as well. The relationship in this respect is largely one-sided. Locality groups get their sponsorship while the companies may attract goodwill but there are limits to how much the drug industry will be willing to pay for this.

2 *Drug purchasing*. Already some groups in Nottingham, for instance, are directly purchasing vaccines as a group. There is the potential for

other agreements of this sort and particularly for group purchasing by dispensing practices within a locality group. Increasingly locality groups are developing their own formularies and trying to get local trusts to sign up to them. This provides a unified prescribing message from the locality and trust and it also reduces some of the eccentricities in prescribing, which may not be based on evidence. It also stops the off-loading of drugs, which are relatively cheap in hospital, into the locality where the drug companies may charge more. It is likely that the pharmaceutical companies will want to become involved in the development of locality formularies and this will pose a conundrum for many LCGs, who are bound to have mixed feelings on this.

3 *Managed care*. It seems that managed care can be used in two ways. In the USA it is used to reduce costs and becomes a restrictive force in what a family physician can do for his or her patient. A result of this has been that some family physicians in America are beginning to form co-operatives not dissimilar from LCGs, which appear to contain costs and maintain standards of care better than the previous top-down managed care systems. In Great Britain, however, managed care has the potential to raise standards uniformly in one or two areas of clinical care where patients did not previously have access to such services. It is likely that GP commissioning groups will experiment with managed care in certain areas as a means of getting trusts and local managers to sign up to certain minimum criteria. This would be fertile ground for the pharmaceutical companies who might wish to become involved in such schemes. For instance, a locality drive, which aimed to target the secondary prevention of coronary artery disease would be based on irrefutable evidence of the benefit of lowering raised cholesterol on patients with previous ischaemic heart disease. Pharmaceutical companies promoting lipid lowering agents might be involved in funding nurse time, IT, cholesterol measuring equipment and administrative assistance to set up guidelines on the appropriate screening for cholesterol levels in target patients. A programme of treatment starting from dietary advice to lipid lowering agents could be devised using nationally agreed standards. There would have to be no coercion or covert pressure on clinicians to prescribe the product promoted by the pharmaceutical company involved. Such an enterprise would need to involve all stakeholders including local cardiologists. The advantage for an LCG in such an example would be that the health of patients in the locality was improved at less expense and without compromising the ethics of all concerned. The money saved could then be used elsewhere.

Many would not subscribe to this scenario as they would say that such a relationship compromises the LCG. They would also say that any short-term gains to a group would be offset in the long term by increased costs to the NHS overall because any help given by drug firms would ultimately be paid in the cost of the drugs themselves and, therefore, by the tax payer. This is an argument, of course, which can be used wherever private enterprise is involved in the NHS including the Private Finance Initiative (PFI) as it presently stands. The difference between locality schemes of this sort and the PFI, however, is that LCGs can remain the senior partner in any such relationship and disengage if they feel that they are being compromised. It is this ability on the part of the local population and its health professionals to have the final say which makes the potential British system crucially different from the American one.

11 Future relationships, functions and needs: a vision for the future

Locality/GP commissioning is now poised to take centre stage in the NHS. It is proving to be both a durable and versatile system. It was invented in many ways as a reaction to the internal market but has rapidly developed and prospered in spite of it. The imminent end of the internal market will not affect the ability of LCGs to continue with all the functions and achievements described in this book. All that is necessary is some division of responsibility between those who decide what services are required and those who provide them. Ron Singer has described GP/locality commissioning as an evolution but it is also a revolution. Some of the likely and possible effects and implications of this revolution as well as its final vision will be examined in this chapter.

Future commissioning groups and their relationship to trusts, health authorities and the centre

Future commissioning groups

GPs are likely to remain at the centre of any future commissioning model. Their global perspective in caring for patients from cradle to grave and their daily contact with individual patients will always ensure this. So will their skills in consulting with others, weighing evidence and pragmatic decision-making. It is too early to say which models of commissioning are likely to provide a template for the future though two elements are likely to be part of the final picture.

(i) *Devolvement of health authority functions to localities.* Some devolvement of health authority functions to locality level in the form of a locality management team seems to be an important means of empowering commissioning groups to achieve their ends. Such a team might include a locality manager, locality purchaser, public health consultant and support staff. Such a team will provide LCGs with the necessary autonomy to make locality plans and liaise directly with trusts and specialists. If a commissioning group wishes it, such a team could also provide it with a co-operative role in making strategic purchasing decisions and in the distribution of the locality budget.

(ii) *Primary care commissioning*. It would be an ideal, if unachievable end point, of locality commissioning if its roots could spread to encompass every patient and health professional within a locality. Towards this ideal it is likely that GP commissioning will give way to primary care commissioning involving other primary care professionals apart from GPs. This will provide commissioning with both a better information base and a much stronger mandate.

The future is likely to see increasing collaboration and sharing of work between neighbouring LCGs. Some commissioning groups are likely to lead on certain health topics and where their work can be replicated this can then be shared with other LCGs saving work and time. The DHA will remain the natural forum for LCGs and their management teams to meet up and integrate commissioning at a district level. 'No man is an Island', however, and commissioning groups are bound to impact on all those around them.

Acute hospital trusts

As the emphasis moves from purchasing to planning, it is likely that commissioning groups will develop plans with specialists across a specialty rather than with each trust. Some groups are already beginning to do this spontaneously (*see* Chapter 6, p. 86). Present day negotiations with acute trusts about the specialist facilities that they are going to provide will give way to direct negotiations with relevant local specialists and could leave acute trusts in the position of sub-contractors providing the necessary back-up facilities for those specialists. Inevitably many acute trusts will become larger in order to avoid duplication of services and to achieve economies of scale. The new partnership of primary and secondary care clinicians would allow them to work together on integrated care pathways between home and hospital and encourage changes in service delivery centred on primary and community settings. The looser link between the specialist and his or her hospital and the reduced emphasis on bricks and mortar should then allow a more patient-centred approach. It would also allay fears that investors in the PFI will dictate the future pace of the NHS.

A health service that is clinically led in this way will be able both to ask the questions and provide the answers. Does it make clinical or financial sense for a young lady with a suspected deep vein thrombosis to linger in a ward bed overnight connected to a heparin drip under the care of junior doctors while waiting for a venogram the next day? Similarly, if acute stroke patients do not receive heparin and a brain scan within an hour of onset (which they do receive in many parts of the USA) is this due to considerations of evidence, cost-effectiveness, resources or simply poor organization? Primary and secondary care physicians will be in a position collectively to challenge historical ways of working and are more likely to find solutions if they feel that they are in control and feel supported rather than threatened by those around them.

Community services provided by trusts

It is possible that more dramatic changes could still occur in the organization of community services. Co-operative planning at present requires the involvement of both the devolved locality team from the health authority and the local trust managers. This duplication may seem increasingly unnecessary as the emphasis moves from purchasing to planning and some primary care commissioning groups may be increasingly tempted to cut out the middle man. The group or even its sub-locality groups might then take on the direct management of community services within a locality themselves. This would also overcome the illogic at present of local health professionals sitting on commissioning boards and discussing purchasing contracts with trust managers who are their employers.

It might seem a little cosy for an LCG both to commission and provide primary services within a locality. Effectively though this is only a quantitative extension from the present situation where GPs are both commissioners and providers. Furthermore, it reflects the situation prior to 1990 when the DHA was responsible for both planning and providing hospital services. In a primary care-led NHS this could be a powerful way of ensuring that community services were locally accountable and of encouraging the appropriate transfer of work from secondary to primary care.

Health authorities

As commissioning groups in association with their locality management teams take over many of the previous responsibilities of DHAs it is likely that the present DHAs will combine to form 'super district health authorities'. This in turn, will obviate the need for a regional outpost for the NHS Executive. With most of their planning and purchasing functions devolved to locality management teams working with LCGs, these super district health authorities will take on a very different role, as described by Jeremy

Hallett in Chapter 1, and become effectively 'health assurance agencies'. In this role, it may be important to ensure that the executive members of a health authority are able to represent fully all the localities covered by commissioning groups. Besides being the local 'OffHealth' monitoring the output of commissioning groups they will also have an on-going role in both developing, supporting and integrating them. They will also maintain an overall strategic role and provide the pathway of financial accountability with the centre.

The centre

It is unlikely that this conceptual revolution will be contained at DHA level. A bottom-up system is bound to affect the top as well. Indeed it is desirable that it should do so. One of the problems of the 'top-down' system that preceded locality commissioning was that the top never really made proper contact with the bottom. The result was the production of unilateral edicts from the top such as the famous three-yearly checks which the 'bottom' carried out with such resentment that these imposed measures were bound to fail. In the 'new system' it will be essential that the bottom can identify with the top – that in some sense at least it should own the top. It will be a further revolution in thinking that will be difficult for those at all levels to grasp and adapt to. Not the case of the tail wagging the dog so much as the tail and the dog beginning to realize that they are, and have always been, part of the same animal. In retrospect it will seem odd to have ever supposed otherwise.

Figure 11.1 illustrates two models of how LCGs and DHAs may become more involved in national decision-making. The involvement of both at the centre reflects the ways in which lead GPs from commissioning groups are becoming involved with DHAs in making decisions at district level. The models offer continuity from top to bottom and both horizontal and vertical accountability. At the bottom, the LCG is accountable to the individual as a patient in the locality. At the top, parliament is accountable to the same individual as a voter and tax payer. Similarly, there need to be GPs at the top of this hierarchy because of the experience that they can bring from the bottom as the result of their individual consultations with those same patients.

Such a system would overcome the dysfunctional hierarchies of the past by incorporating the best of the present vertical system with the horizontal and co-operative working procedures that are commonly seen in primary care. The concept of national decisions being made collectively by all stakeholders in the NHS with primary care representation at the top has to be a long-term aim for a primary care-led NHS. If some commissioning

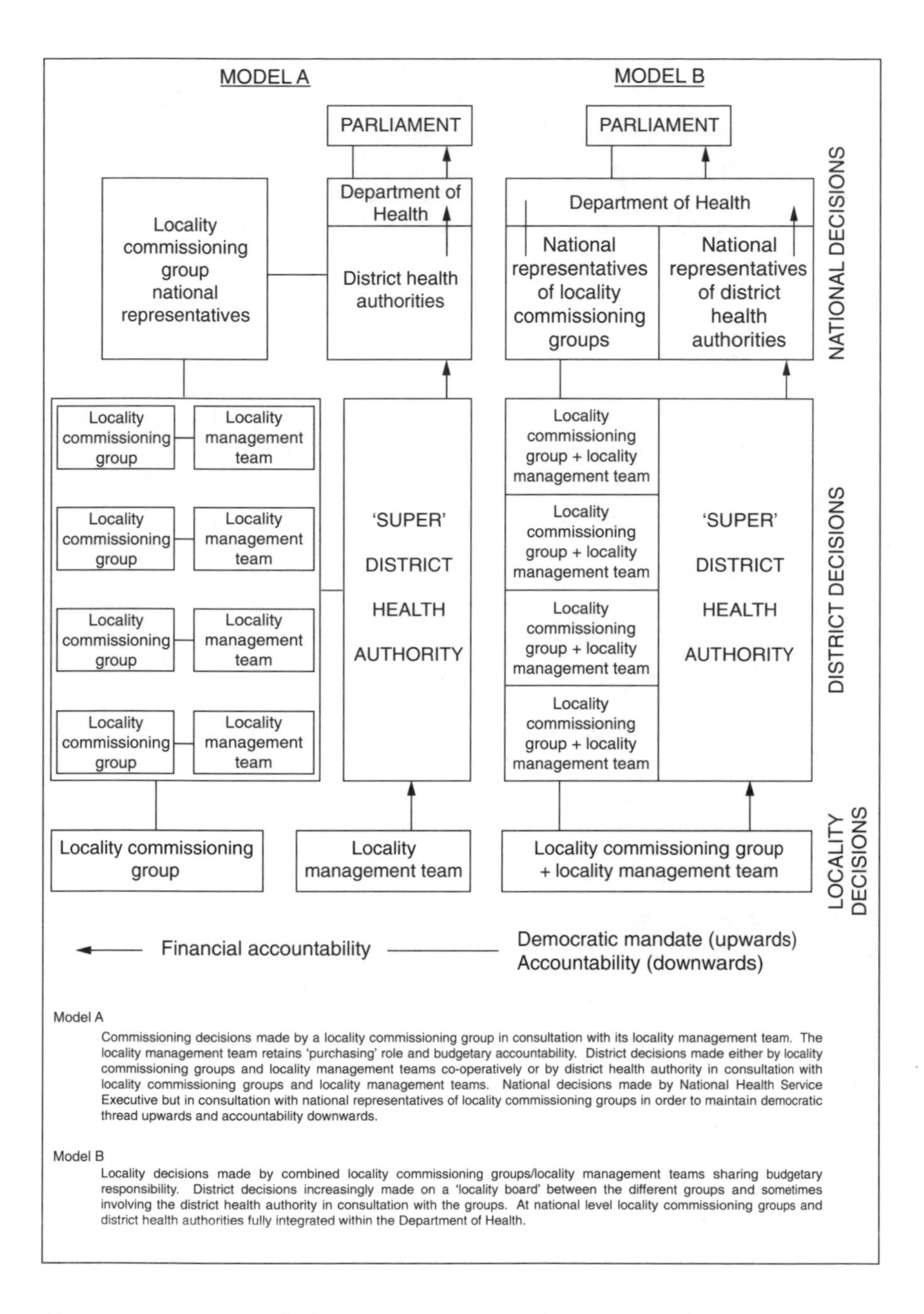

Figure 11.1: Connecting the bottom to the top – two future models of locality commissioning.

groups are to take on increased co-operative budgetary responsibility then it follows that they should provide increased central input. As far as the GPs themselves are concerned, they would receive *pro rata* payments for carrying out this advanced commissioning role and as individual GPs they could receive negotiated payment for any non-core services that they offered. Meanwhile the provision of core general medical services could continue to be entirely separate and beyond the remit of commissioning groups.

Future roles

LCGs will have their work cut out for the time being as they begin to grapple with the work outlined in this book. The next few years will see LCGs concentrating on producing comprehensive and integrated local health strategies and taking on the processes of needs assessment and audit. Some groups will be looking at the concept of sharing budgetary responsibility with the health authority as a means of seeing if resources can be more easily transferred between different aspects of secondary care and between secondary and primary care itself. All this work is likely to be done within a culture of increasing relative financial shortage which will further challenge the inventiveness of LCGs, health authorities and trusts. Given the immensity of this task, LCGs will not be looking for extended roles, nevertheless an increasing recognition of their potential will lead to new tasks.

Improving the standards of general practice and primary care

Commissioning groups will inevitably become involved in this area because decisions by GPs on whether to prescribe, refer, diagnose and treat are of fundamental importance in explaining how resources are used. Unless a framework is created for influencing and changing the decisions of doctors and other staff then the aspiration to modernize and improve the NHS will remain empty rhetoric.

Locality commissioning provides a focus for clinical decision-making and, as we have seen throughout this book, commissioning groups are evolving as a major force for improving the quality of general practice. The basis for this role has been the close contact, trust and mutual co-operation between practices within the commissioning process. The catalyst has been the realization that the role of groups in commissioning secondary care is intimately related with the problem of how primary and secondary care physicians can improve the interface between the two and ultimately the quality of primary care itself. The result has been the production of jointly agreed guidelines and referral procedures which have improved the quality of both secondary and primary care. Increasingly, groups are working towards locality guidelines for work in primary care such as the secondary prevention of coronary artery disease and are involving practices in locality audits (*see* Chapter 8) to see if they have achieved their ends. The essence of success has been the ability to inspire all practices in a locality to accept non-threatening peer pressure.

Education and peer pressure are probably the only effective ways to change practice. Not surprisingly, therefore, centrally driven government directives such as the new GP contract have had only marginal effect upon general practice itself. The rates of cervical smears and immunizations may be higher but the evidence suggests that measures such as health promotion clinics had minimum impact as far as the average patient was concerned. A brave attempt to upgrade the worse practices resulted in the homogenization and frequent demoralization of many of the better ones without fundamentally changing worst practice. There is no reason to believe that Department of Health imposed performance indicators will be any more successful than previous attempts to bring about 'top-down' solutions.

The Royal College of General Practitioners has taken a vital leading role in improving education in general practice, which has undoubtedly raised standards. At present, however, its active membership at locality level is not sufficient to provide a comprehensive network of peer pressure. Some GPs, particularly those who may need help and support in improving their practices, feel that the Royal College is remote and threatening. Local medical committees have taken on some of this work in the past but may be compromised in some areas by their other roles. LCGs also have the advantage of working closely with locality management teams and DHAs, which can support and authenticate their work in this area.

To date, this work has focused on improving standards of clinical care. Increasing trust and co-operation between practices could in future allow the process to develop on a much more fundamental level of looking at, for instance, standards in the consultation and assessing in more depth the subjective and objective impact that practices have upon their patient population. Those concerned will need to understand and respect the heterogeneity of general practice and develop models which explain the popularity and therapeutic efficacy of some GPs who appear to defy any evidence base.

Research

The wealth of available information (*see* Chapter 8) and the collective enthusiasm available within localities could provide a future base for both originating and disseminating research. If so, it would be important to stimulate and commission good quality appropriate research in the localities to balance the increasing centralization of research commissioning towards regional and national levels. Indeed, research could proceed along the lines of Figure 11.1 being commissioned at national, regional (super district health authority) and locality level. Localities will need the appropriate skills as well as the appropriate financial resources and the former could be provided by local centres of research excellence in very much the same way as audit skills are presently being provided by primary care audit groups as described in Chapter 8. Enabling localities to commission, conduct and utilize research in this way will not only impact on patient care but it will also offer every GP access to research. An enabling process that can only improve the attractiveness and morale of general practice itself.

Rationing

The rationing question for most GPs means – 'Will we have to keep within budgets?' As we have seen (*see* Chapter 7) commissioning groups have at least four options in this respect. They can leave all budgetary decisions entirely to their locality management team, they can offer advice to the locality team on budgetary issues, they can share this responsibility with the locality management team or they can 'go it alone'. The question of who actually holds the budget has become a bit of a non-issue and there is no point in a group choosing the last option if its locality management team is up to standard and the DHA have allowed them sufficient independence. Conversely, few commissioning groups are likely to choose the first option and leave it all entirely to their locality management team because the handling of the budget will be a crucial part of how and which plans come to fruition. Consequently, it is very likely that most commissioning groups will either be happy to offer advice on the distribution of a budget or, as in the case of the Nottingham Total Commissioning Pilot, accept shared budgetary responsibility with the health authority or its locality management team. Whatever the arrangement, health authorities must listen but commissioning groups must accept some degree of responsibility and ownership. Furthermore, commissioning groups must never be made to accept financial responsibility nor should any doctors who choose this option have any personal financial interest in doing so.

Accepting budgetary responsibility does not, as Ron Singer has pointed out, mean accepting a rationing role. It means accepting an enhanced role in prioritizing services and, as we have seen, setting priorities is very much a part of commissioning. The rationing role proper is the province of those who fix the level of the budgets in the first place. Locality commissioning will, however, enable the rationing process to become much more transparent (*see* Chapter 4). Within the fundholding model it was theoretically possible both to devolve and hide the rationing question and there was a theoretical incentive for GPs to collude in this process. Within the commissioning model, if a commissioning group says that it cannot afford vital services, then the health authority will need to show it how it can or both will need to confront the problem at a higher level. As far as the Treasury is concerned, it probably does not matter whether commissioning groups, locality management teams or both are financially responsible. As far as patients and local services are concerned it may be as desirable as some think it is inevitable that groups will take on some of this role.

Future requirements

Locality commissioning is a cheap option but it will fail if it is run 'on the cheap'. GPs, whether they are involved at the level of the practice, the board or as lead GPs, will all need adequate remuneration appropriate for the task. This will also encourage the less enthusiastic to join in the task. If the level of funding is appropriate then this should be sufficient to expect commissioning groups to perform. An added incentive for those involved in GP commissioning will be the ability to see local services improving and to vire resources into the most important areas for service provision. GPs will also need to be offered adequate training. There will be debate as to whether GPs should also receive performance-related pay for their involvement and whether resources could be vired into individual practices and services provided by them. The danger of either is that the 'post-Gorbachev' era of the NHS could then be in danger of being run by medical spivs. The alternative of adequately remunerating both general medical services and work spent on locality commissioning seems preferable.

At present most LCGs and the locality management teams they work with rely upon their DHA to provide for their management costs and personnel. It is presently unclear how much it costs to devolve health authority functions in this way and many would say that it is cost neutral. Nevertheless, in as much as fundholders have received direct payment from central funds for their management costs, it is only logical that locality management teams and commissioning groups should also receive central funding and support. In some commissioning groups, practice managers and fundholding managers are becoming involved and fundholders within such groups are beginning to share resources, particularly IT, with the rest of their group. Such initiatives provide an evolutionary lead for the transfer of resources from fundholding into commissioning.

Finally, as we have seen (*see* Chapter 8), commissioning groups and particularly their non-fundholding practices will need proper funding for IT. The future should see electronic links becoming the norm in every practice and practice morbidity data becoming a vital part of each locality health strategy.

It is remarkable that locality commissioning has developed so far with so little central support and funding. More will be needed in the future for it to meet its potential and for it to engender the interest of all GPs and health professionals.

Conclusion

Locality commissioning is not just another structural alteration. It represents the greatest change in philosophy since the beginning of the NHS. It bids a final farewell to the benign paternalistic system in which patients were supposed to feel grateful for what was sometimes a substandard service. It heralds a more accountable service which no longer depends upon an outdated hierarchy but which is a function of a new co-operative involvement and commitment.

GP/locality commissioning is the only model in recent years to provide an all inclusive and comprehensive vision of the future. All inclusive because all patients, GPs, allied professionals, specialists, managers from health authorities and trusts and finally the NHSE itself can be actively involved. Comprehensive because it provides the building blocks for a complete model of the NHS, which for the first time links the bottom to the top and back again. It is a vision of an integrated service where services are integrated at locality level, between primary and secondary care and between the locality, the district and the Department of Health. Finally, it is a vision that bridges the divide between fundholder and non-fundholder, between GPs and health authorities and between GPs and other health professionals, trusts and local authorities.

At locality level, the vision is of a locality strategy, which is owned collectively by patients, GPs, other health professionals and managers, and which includes all the relevant services such as social services and housing. A locality infrastructure of this kind cannot only provide a balanced view of how to improve the health of a locality but also a seamless system for delivering it. No longer need confused elderly patients with poor mobility fall between health and social services. No longer should a patient with respiratory disease be given expensive drugs in isolation from his or her greater need for adequate damp proofing, heating or ground floor accommodation. Within such a locality, all those involved will take responsibility for the resulting health services as part and parcel of being able to shape them in the first place. Prioritizing services will undoubtedly become important, especially when money is scarce, and common responsibility in this process may lead to a corporate ownership of some difficult health decisions. This may prevent some of the more emotional, knee-jerk reactions, which the press has traditionally supported and to which politicians have traditionally succumbed. The future is also likely to see a changing role for local authorities with the establishment of joint budgets and joint agencies for some groups of patients such as the mentally ill.

As commissioning groups take on many of the previous functions of a DHA, these are likely to become enlarged 'super district health authorities' covering much larger populations and with reduced management costs. Co-ordination of commissioning activity outside each locality will sometimes involve relevant commissioning groups commissioning together and sometimes require co-ordination of such activities at the level of the 'super health authority'. The health authority will remain financially accountable but will also be responsible for ensuring that its commissioning groups can take on central directives and are performing adequately. Trusts will undergo a similar process of enlargement but the focus of communication will become GP commissioner to specialist rather than GP commissioner to trust. This will allow an integration of primary and secondary care and a new generation of hospital doctors who can relate directly to patients and local GPs and with a looser relationship and commitment to the equipment, bricks and mortar, which will be contracted to support them. In this way commissioning will harness the expertise and commitment of both primary and secondary care clinicians and allow them to work together on integrated care pathways between home and hospital.

The vision offers equity of care to all patients and also equality of funding to doctors and commissioning groups involved in the process. The output is unlikely to be equal as localities will vary in their needs and commissioning groups will vary in their success in meeting those needs. The inequalities that do occur may have the positive effect of encouraging commissioning groups to try and match each other's performance in an upward direction as they will all be starting from the same point.

There will be a move towards co-ownership of problems rather than answers being imposed by a hierarchical structure. Never again should GPs be ordered to check the height of each patient every three years or be financially encouraged to offer health promotion facilities of unproven worth. Central directives will always remain necessary but these should become less the despised orders from above but instead take the form of negotiated decisions between the centre and the periphery. In the 'primary care-led NHS' of the future it is inevitable that this should be so. General practice and primary health care teams rely on mutual support, co-operation and respect. They are quite unlike the hierarchical structures that occur in hospitals and health authorities. The great experiment will be to see if the same structures that have made British general practice the jewel in the crown of the modern NHS are generalizable.

Two questions will remain. Firstly, are GPs either able or willing to take on such a great co-operative venture? The scale of the task should not be underestimated as GPs have limited experience of working in collectives bigger than a partnership and will need to develop the skills and be given the training to do so. Secondly, will the NHS Executive entrust tax payer's money to commissioning groups or the locality managers delegated by health authorities to work with them? GPs will clearly need reassurances about individual clinical autonomy while the NHSE will require a satisfactory accountability framework. Locality commissioning is not without its risks – risks to GPs, consultants, trusts, the NHSE, the government and not to mention the very patient who is at the centre of this process. Any great change involves risks but in this case they are relatively small and the benefits for all are inestimable. GP commissioning, it must be remembered, is a product of convergent evolution involving many groups representing all types of communities around the country. It was not a political solution to a funding crisis but the result of a widespread desire to make things better and to make the best use of what is available. The NHS is at a crossroads and in desperate need of a new common vision. GP commissioners and health authority managers throughout Great Britain are in the process of creating just such a vision.

Appendix 1: National Association of Commissioning GPs

Purpose

To promote and support the involvement of all GPs in the equitable commissioning of high quality care for their patients, within the context of a wider population.

Aims

- To support existing commissioning groups
- To encourage the formation of new commissioning groups
- To develop models of effective and efficient utilization of resources
- To disseminate information and share experience within the NHS
- To monitor the effectiveness of the processes we promote
- To lobby at local and national levels for recognition, finance and protected time for GP involvement.

How can the NACGP help?

- We hold a continually expanding database of most of the established and emergent commissioning groups in the UK and can provide details of groups in your area
- We have produced a *Directory of GP Commissioning Groups* that contains much useful information about the structure and functioning of nearly 60 different groups
- We can put you in touch with other GPs in your area who have expressed an interest in commissioning but do not have a local group

- We hold a register of doctors who can speak publicly on commissioning issues and can often help at initial founding meetings
- The NACGP executive is collecting data on various models of commissioning and can put you in touch with groups using these models
- The NACGP holds workshops on commissioning topics at its Annual and Extraordinary Meetings
- We are happy to receive any queries relating to commissioning, and will try to find a solution or at least put you in touch with a helpful contact.

Membership of the NACGP

The National Association of Commissioning GPs is open to membership by individual GPs or practices (either fundholding or non-fundholding), commissioning groups and other organizations such as health authorities/ commissions. The annual membership fees are as follows:

Individual GPs or practices	£10
Commissioning groups	£50
Other organizations, e.g. health authorities	£250

Membership of the association entitles you to access to advice and support in matters relating to the commissioning process as well as a *Directory of GP Commissioning Groups*.

You will also receive a regular newsletter, contributed to by the membership, if there is a continuing demand and support for such a service.

An application form to join the Association is obtainable from:

Dr Alan Birchall, Secretary, NACGP, Red Lion Cottage, 228 High Road, Chilwell, Nottingham NG9 5DB. Please send a SAE.

Appendix 2: Contractual Agreement 1995/96 between Exeter and North Devon Health Authority and the Mid-Devon General Practitioner Group

Contract details

This document is to formalize the arrangement whereby Exeter and North Devon Health Authority agrees to pay the Mid-Devon GP Group for the following areas of work.

1. **General**

1.1 *Aims and Objectives*

The overall aim of the Mid-Devon GP Group will be to provide a unified approach for the purchase and provision of health care in Mid-Devon seeking to ensure that the local population is provided with high quality health care.

Within its overall aims, the Mid-Devon GP Group has identified three key areas which will underpin its involvement in the work undertaken. These are as follows:

1.2 *Development of a locality health strategy*

The Mid-Devon GP Group will work in partnership with the locality purchasing officer to develop a local strategy for the commissioning of health and health care services.

1.3 *Monitoring of performance*

Recognizing the opportunity to ensure that health care services reflect the needs of GPs and their patients, the Mid-Devon GP Group will be actively involved in the shaping and monitoring of health care contract performance. A key challenge will be to ensure that commissioned services concentrate on improving the quality and effectiveness of patient treatment.

1.4 *Development of the Mid-Devon GP Group towards implementing the recommendations of EL(94)74:* Towards a Primary Care-led NHS Promote and develop the Mid-Devon GP Group's active involvement in commissioning of all health service requirements for the local population on behalf of the health authority.

2. **Workload**
   - Monthly executive meeting
   - Quarterly meeting of Mid-Devon GP Group
   - Approximately 1 to 2 monthly meetings with the locality purchasing officer.

3. **Specific tasks**
   The following areas of locality purchasing work will be developed and implemented during 1995/96.

3.1 Identify all community health services purchased for the locality (resource financial investment, 'what' service provided)

3.2 Develop practice level agreements to enable each GP practice to determine exact nature of community health service purchased on behalf of their population

3.3 Progress discussions with SSD district manager around the development of practice level agreements for social care services

3.4 Development of local hospital discharge protocols and specification

3.5 Explore options for purchasing services with a view to shifting work to alternative providers where appropriate. Consideration in 1995/96 to be undertaken with regard to the following work:
   - arthroscopies
   - ENT
   - eye outpatients surgery

3.6 Establish audit as an integral function of the Mid-Devon GP Group locality purchasing work

3.7 Develop locality health strategy, commissioning plans and accountability framework for Mid-Devon GP Group

3.8 Identify information technology (IT) needs to develop efficient locality purchasing and contract performance feeding into commissions overall information technology strategy.

4. **Payment**

4.1 Invoices for payment are to be forwarded directly to the health authority, with a copy for the secretary of the group.

Type of contract: non-recurring

Value of contract in	1995/96
Executive group @ £---- pa × 5 executive members	£--------
GP representatives on Mid-Devon Group @ £---- pa × number of practices	£--------
Secretarial expenses @ £---- per hour ---- hours per week	£--------
Total:	£--------

AGREED START DATE: ____________

CONTRACT VALID UNTIL: ____________

SIGNED ON BEHALF OF MID-DEVON GROUP	SIGNED ON BEHALF OF HEALTH AUTHORITY
....	....
Dated	Dated ....

Appendix 3: Suggested final agreement between a commissioning group and its health authority*

Aim of the agreement:

- to seek recognition of the need to involve GPs and provider clinicians at all stages of the commissioning process
- to reinforce and facilitate the role of a representative group of GPs contracted to advise the commissioning process outside their clinical commitment.

The commissioning group will:

- aim to be representative of GP opinion
- undertake to put issues into context, recognizing the external constraints affecting the health authority
- aim to develop mechanisms to identify problems and assist in providing solutions to health care delivery.

The health authority will:

- act on advice and recommendations from the group or give reasons in writing when advice or recommendations are not followed
- make available public health, planning and purchasing information
- present issues in time for GP consideration and response
- ensure the involvement of the group in the health authority's relationship with providers
- ensure realistic funding based on the extent of GP time required
- set and maintain standards for meetings involving GPs

* From Singer R (ed.) (1997) *GP Commissioning: an inevitable evolution*. Radcliffe Medical Press, Oxford.

- promote the involvement of the group by inducting their staff in the group's role and remit.

The group and the health authority will jointly:

- aim to co-produce an annual commissioning strategy for the area
- agree a work programme for commissioning based on a rolling five-year cycle
- hold regular policy meetings
- actively contribute towards effective relationships with all GPs regardless of fundholding status
- actively strive to promote each other's interests in relation to the commissioning process and in ways that benefit the local community.

Appendix 4: An example of a constitution – Huddersfield GP Commissioning Group

1. Group shall be known as HGPCG.
2. All GPs with practices in Huddersfield postcode district are automatically members of HGPCG.
3. Committee to consist of nine elected representatives.
4. Each committee member to represent similar number of GPs. This will mean some postal code areas have two representatives whilst others share one.
5. It is not necessary for a committee member to have surgery premises in postcode area represented.
6. Each committee member is responsible for canvassing opinion from its constituency membership and for conveying these views to the executive and committee.
7. A copy of the mission statement, aims and objectives and constitution shall be sent to all members.
8. Executive will comprise two joint co-ordinators who will be responsible for day-to-day responsibilities and co-ordinating activity. Either of these will act as chair at committee meetings.
9. Executive and committee are responsible for ensuring that constitution is strictly adhered to.
10. Committee and executive to serve a three-yearly term:
    - one-third be offered for election annually
    - members of committee to be elected at AGM by those present
    - method of election: ballot
      - nominations for each constituency to be received no later than 14 days prior to AGM

- constituents to elect their own representative only
- joint co-ordinators and officers to be re-elected annually by the committee.

In the event of no nominations being received for a committee member, the residing member for that area shall be returned unopposed.

11 Should a seat on the committee be vacated for any reason, the executive committee and committee can elect another member to service, whose term of office stands until the following AGM.

12 Decisions taken at committee level, should be voted in by a majority. In the event of a tie, the chair to have the casting vote.

13 A quorum shall consist of the chair or nominee, plus four committee members.

14 Executive and committee have right to co-opt a member on to the committee to handle special tasks as defined by them. The holder of appointment created in this manner would have no voting rights on the committee and would not normally attend committee meetings unless specifically requested to do so.

15 The committee has the power to suspend a fellow committee member who in the view of the full committee has seriously contravened the constitution or brought the HGPCG into disrepute. This power to also apply if a member has not attended a meeting for three months without an apology being sent.

16 The AGM is to be held on the first Wednesday in November.

17 Notice convening the meeting shall be sent to every member not less than 28 days before the date of the AGM.

18 Constitutional rules open to amendment by the members at the AGM.

19 A special meeting of members shall be called by the secretary on receipt of a request in writing signed by no fewer than ten constituency members.

20 An auditor shall be appointed but would not hold office or be a member of the committee.

Index